Little Green Kitchen

Little Green Kitchen

Simple vegetarian family recipes

DAVID FRENKIEL & LUISE VINDAHL

Hardie Grant

BOOKS

DEDICATION

To all parents. You are doing a great job. Just hang in there.

And to our children, Elsa, Isac and Noah. The bravest, kindest and strongest little humans we know.

May our post-dinner wrestling tradition never end.

Contents

INTRODUCTION

I had just finished cooking a Tofu cashew masala (page 43) for dinner and was feeling pretty proud of myself and my Indian stew. It had a round and sweet scent with just the right amount of spices to suit the kids, and was mixed super-smooth with only pieces of tofu floating on top. This had been one of our eight-year-old's favourite meals throughout the summer – we even have a cute shot of her holding a bowl of masala in this book (page 42). But when she entered the kitchen she took only one glimpse at the stove before bursting into tears:

'We had terrible lunch at school and now I'm coming home TO THIS!? I'm so hungry but I haaaate stews. Why are you doing this to meeeeeee!?'

The road to feeding your children isn't always straight. We know this all too well. We have three children between two and eight years old who we have raised on a mainly vegetarian diet. There are days when plates end up on the floor, when you have to bribe and bargain, when you've spent hours in the kitchen cooking for your family only to end up serving the kids a cheese sandwich or a bowl of oats because they are refusing to eat anything else. But there are good days too. Days when they pour down smoothies spiked with cauliflower, avocado or beetroot (beet) (page 136) and ask for refills; when a tray of Middle Eastern roasted broccoli (page 36) or Green bean fries (page 47) are gone before we even had time to sit down; when their mouths are filled with Spinach and cottage cheese waffles (page 31) and when, on weekends, they help us stuff Tomatoes with black rice (page 80).

There are many things in parenthood that aren't easy, but if there is one task worth a little extra effort, it's your children's food and health, wouldn't you agree? That is why we wrote this book: to share what we have learned through writing four (this is our fifth) vegetarian cookbooks while raising three young children. We want to give recipes, tools and tips to parents on how to cook wholesome and vegetable-focused food for their family. But, also, to tell you that it's okay when all bowls aren't licked clean. You still did a great job and it will pay off in the future (see page 23 for more on this).

We asked our daughter if she would feel better eating that cashew masala while drawing, on a tray in her bed. She nodded, still sobbing. Thirty minutes and three Pokémon drawings later she asked for a third bowl of masala. You see, if there is one thing we have learned through all of this, it is that many outbursts aren't even about the food. A thought that is equal parts comforting and hopeless.

OUR FAMILY AND FOOD

This year marks the ten-year anniversary since Luise and I launched our blog Green Kitchen Stories (woohoo!) and started this journey of cooking and writing recipes together. Our family has grown and we have evolved through the years, but the essence of our recipes and food philosophy is still the same. Our recipes are always centred around vegetables. But also wholegrains, good fats, natural sweeteners, nuts, seeds, pulses (legumes) and fruit.

We try to have a positive and relaxed approach to healthy food and we truly believe that by eating well we can all feel better.

We have brought up our children – Elsa, currently eight, Isac, currently four, and Noah, currently two – on a mainly vegetarian diet, meaning that they eat what we eat. I have been a vegetarian for over 20 years. Luise is not, but at home she eats 90 per cent vegetarian food with the add-in of fish dishes for her and the kids every now and then. The boys' preschool is a fantastic little place where they only serve homemade organic vegetarian food, and we have actually picked up a couple of ideas from them that we have included in this book. Elsa eats vegetarian food and fish at her school. Their health has always been our main goal and if we for one second felt that they wouldn't get all the nutrients they needed from their diet, we would re-evaluate our choices. They are, however, three happy, wild and strong little humans, so we continue down this path for now.

As the kids are growing they have been gaining more influence on our cooking. There is more hand-held food, more cheese (hello halloumi!), more pasta and other comfort food coming out of our kitchen nowadays. You'll notice that in this book as well. We take more shortcuts with store-bought vegetable patties or tofu sausages when we don't have the time or energy to make our own. The way we see it, all shortcuts that help you and your family stay sane are welcome – just check the ingredient lists to avoid too many weird substances and unnecessary added sugars.

We teach our kids about how vegetables make us strong. How desserts make us happy. And that we need a good mix of both. We often finish each dinner with a wrestling match, a running competition or an arm wrestle. It's a simple and fun demonstration of how strong the food we eat makes us. I'll stuff a few extra spinach leaves or beans in my mouth before leaving the table to make sure I can beat them. And then they do the same, because they want to beat me. It is a playful approach to health and I think our kids realise that it's not exactly how it works. But as long as I lose, they're happy.

THIS BOOK

We don't cook separate meals for our children and this book is not an exception. Who has the time and energy to cook double dinners anyway? This is a cookbook for families. With fun, modern, wholesome and vegetable-focused meals created with kids' palates in mind, but which are also interesting enough for adults to enjoy. All main meals have upgrade suggestions for adults at the end of each recipe. They are ideas for how to make them spicier, greener, more flavour-packed, or to add textures to a dish and toppings to a soup (of course, you can also serve the upgrades to your kids if you think they will like them).

So, with little or no alteration the same meal will feed the entire family.

A HELPING HAND

We believe that involving children in the kitchen is essential. Therefore, most recipes have a section called 'A helping hand' (except for the ones in the Condiments and Upgrades chapter), where we suggest what the kids can help out with. It can be chopping softer ingredients (small children are less likely to slip and cut themselves on tofu and (bell) pepper than pumpkin and carrots), stirring sauces, decorating and tasting the food. Some of these tips might seem obvious, but see them as reminders to include children in the kitchen. Even if it can take a little longer with them stirring the pots or playing 'it's snowing!' with a bag of flour, you are doing them a huge favour. Not forgetting that it makes them more invested in the food, which multiplies the chances of them actually eating it.

TALK ABOUT FOOD

Our hope is that you use this as more than just a recipe book. We want it to be a sort of conversation starter between you and your child/children. Talk about food, talk about vegetables, about fruit, fast food, school meals, how vegetables taste and how they grow. Help them understand why you want them to try something new. Don't focus on good or bad food. Describe food as something that will help their bodies grow, give them energy, make them stronger, happier, faster, smarter. To get you started, we have listed questions in all chapter openers about vegetables and food. Questions that don't really have a right or wrong answer, but instead will get them (and you) thinking. Questions such as: *How many colours have you eaten today?*

THE RECIPES

The majority of recipes in this book focus on everyday meals because that's what parents seem to struggle most with. Try our Roasted veg soup with halloumi croûtons (page 68), which delivers maximum flavour with minimal effort, or our take on a classic spaghetti carbonara but with parsnip and courgette (zucchini) (page 63). There is a chapter with party food that features more playful dishes that can be fun to make on weekends or when you have friends over. Like the Butternut börek snake (page 94) that looks like an impossible thing to make but actually isn't. We also have a chapter with lunchbox ideas, recipes and small treats that travel well in a backpack. Give our Crispy rice paper rolls (page 125) a try, or the PB hummus and carrot flatbread rolls (page 118). The lunchbox recipes are all pretty fun and cute and could also work for quick dinners, so make sure to check them out. We love to snack and have dedicated a chapter to smoothies, bowls, bars and savoury muffins in order to give you better options than handing a candy bar or a bag of chips to your kids. Quick tips and treats that taste great and will keep you energised until dinner. There is a chapter with condiments and upgrades. Make sure you try the Chocolate chickpea spread (page 166) and our super-simple Berry and chia jams (page 161).

Our dessert chapter has some epic sweets, cookies, shakes and birthday cakes that taste fantastic. Even in this chapter, we have spiked many of the recipes with vegetables and use natural sweeteners throughout. We do eat normal sugary desserts every now and then, but we're pretty sure you didn't buy this book to learn how to make a classic brownie. We'll let other books be good at that, and we will instead teach you how to make a delicious brownie with black beans (page 176) or a sweet roll-up cake with beetroot (beet) (page 187).

All the recipes have been tested – not only by us and our children, as well as our assistant Sophie – but also by our tester, Nic, working from a kitchen in New Zealand on the other side of the world from us. That way, we could make sure the recipes work and taste good, regardless of where you live.

We cross all our fingers that this book will be helpful for your family's cooking endeavours. We know how challenging little mouths can be to feed and we want to be there for you. Your children probably won't love every dish in the book but hopefully you will find a few new family favourites, just as we have while writing this.

Loads of love from us!

David, Luise, Elsa, Isac and Noah

HOW TO FEED YOUR FAMILY MORE VEGETABLES

Wouldn't it be amazing if we could invent a magical pill that could make children eat all their vegetables, clear their plates after dinner, never wake their parents in the mornings and only ask for ice cream and cookies on Saturdays? How easy life would be for us. Well, we don't have that pill yet. But what we have instead is this list. Here we have gathered all our thoughts, tips and methods on how to get your little (and big) ones to try new flavours and eat more greens.

1. START EARLY
This obviously won't help anyone with older children, but if you have a baby, try to give him or her proper food (when they start on solid food). Focus on a variety of vegetables, wholegrains (cooked and puréed) and not too much sweet food too early. You'll make it easier for yourself later on.

2. CRANK UP THE HEAT
Roasting vegetables and roots on a high heat in the oven gives them a char, a sweet caramelisation and that crunchy-on-the-outside-but-soft-in-the-middle texture that many children like. Check out the recipes on pages 28, 36 and 68.

3. VEGGIE-BOOST FOOD THAT YOU KNOW THEY LIKE
Blend spinach or carrots and add to pancakes; mix quinoa into burger patties or sneak lentils into their favourite pasta sauce.

4. DIVIDE AND CONQUER!
Instead of putting a big salad or a mixed vegetable pasta on the table, try a tapas approach using the same ingredients. A lot of children like to eat one thing at a time. Divide the foods into separate bowls and watch your children conquer new ingredients that they never would have tried if they were mixed into a salad.

5. ADD FAT
Most vegetables don't carry fat so by combining them with cheese, olive oil, nuts etc., they taste better, become more comforting, flavourful and filling. Grate a little cheese over asparagus, add an extra glug of olive oil to a soup, mix nut butter into a green smoothie.

6. TOP WITH CINNAMON

Spices can be tricky around many (Western) kids but one spice that often works is cinnamon. It has a friendly, sweet taste that can be paired with lots of vegetables to improve the flavour of the dish and make the vegetable flavours less prominent. Try sprinkling it over a tray of roasted cauliflower, on kale chips or in a sweet potato curry.

7. RAINBOW FOOD

Vegetables are natural colouring agents. Use them to make food more playful and fun! Bread, pancakes, soups, dumplings and spreads can all be tinted beetroot (beet) pink, spinach green, tomato red and carrot orange.

8. MIX IT UP

Many children are doubtful about chunky textures, so a smooth sauce or soup is often more welcome. A hand-held blender is your best friend for this. It's also a great tool for mixing/hiding extra vegetables into simple sauces and soups.

9. PICK YOUR FIGHTS

This has nothing to do with cooking but if you focus on having a positive vibe around the table, it is usually a lot easier to get kids to try new foods. When they are already tired and cranky, new food will just be another reason to fight. We sometimes let our kids eat under the table, inside the pantry or with their hands instead of a knife and fork if that means that they are giving new food a chance. Arguably, they aren't great at table manners, but we'd rather have them eating well than knowing how to hold a fork properly.

10. INVISIBLE VEG

Smoothies are great for hiding vegetables. There are plenty of things you can add to them – look for packs of frozen spinach, broccoli, courgettes (zucchini) and cauliflower in the supermarket. Most of them are already steamed or precooked and can therefore go straight into smoothies. Beetroots (beets) and carrots can be grated into smoothies raw, and avocados can be used to get a lovely thick texture. You can even add cooked white beans to smoothies; their flavour and texture will be disguised by the sweetness from the fruit. Check out page 136 for three veggie-packed smoothie recipes.

11. NO TOUCHING

For some reason, most children don't like it when one food touches another food on their plate. So, serving their food on plates with separate compartments is a way to give them a variety of food and then let them eat it the way they feel comfortable with.

12. SAME BUT DIFFERENT

If your child doesn't like a specific vegetable, try a different cooking technique, chop it differently or add it to a soup. Vegetables are like chameleons and can change a lot depending on how they're cooked. A boiled broccoli can be rather bland to chew on but roasted has an entirely different texture and flavour.

13. HUNGER GAMES

Kids often come asking for food 30 minutes before dinner is ready. Instead of giving them a sandwich or treat, this is an excellent opportunity to put a tray of raw vegetable sticks on the table. When they are hungry, they are more likely to give new vegetables a try and, because vegetable sticks are not very filling, they will still have room left for dinner.

14. FIRST CHIEF PLANNER

Let the children help with planning the weekly dinners. When they are invested, the chances are higher that they will also eat the food. Set some basic rules for the dinner schedule. For example: soup one day, pasta one day, pancake one day etc., and then let them decide the type of pasta, sauce, soup etc. Talk about colours and what's in season and steer them surreptitiously to make sure that you get a variety each week.

15. HOW WAS IT?

Letting children taste the food while it's cooking is a simple trick, but asking for their opinion actually helps. Let them know what they should be looking for: Does it need more salt? Should we add a little sweetness? Do you want to squeeze some lemon into it? Maybe we could mix this sauce smoother? It will teach them to formulate more helpful opinions/feedback than just the common 'I don't like the food'.

16. THE NAKED CARROT

This is one of our favourite little tricks. It is ridiculously simple but it has increased our carrot intake by 500 per cent. Buy the largest pack of carrots you can find and peel them all in one go (preferably in front of Netflix if you get bored easily). Then put them in a large bowl or jar, covered in water, and place in the refrigerator. Now the kids can help themselves whenever they ask for something to chew on. Having naked carrots ready to just put on the table when the kids are home from school makes all the difference. And the water helps keep them fresh and prevents them from drying out.

17. IT'S NOT POISON

Being hesitant towards new food is actually a survival instinct. So it's not an all-bad thing. Think of it as though your kid is unconsciously trying to make sure that you are not poisoning them. Be a good example and show them how good it tastes by sitting down and eating it yourself. If you or your partner won't eat the food, your child surely won't either. Also, keep putting it there and after a while it won't be as scary any more.

18. PLAY THE LONG GAME

One mantra that we believe in fully is to not be too short-sighted in your cooking endeavours. Your child doesn't have to eat everything on the table. Simply placing beans and salad and sauerkraut on the dinner table has an important function that many parents don't even reflect on. It educates your children and shows them what it is, how it is served and eaten. And eventually they will also know how it tastes. But if you stop serving them food they don't like, they definitely won't know what it is and you take away the opportunity for them to say yes to it one day. It might seem like a thankless task, but it can also be a comforting thought if not all the bowls were licked. At least you are widening their perspective on food.

RECIPE NOTES

Regardless of how much detail we include in a recipe, it will not be the same dish in your kitchen. Vegetables vary in size, flavour and texture depending on season, ripeness and where they have been growing. Oven temperatures vary and kale chips that take only 10 minutes for us might need 13 minutes in your oven. We have tried to make these recipes as easy and yet instructive as possible, but we do ask that you taste and season before you serve, and feel free to substitute an ingredient if it's not in season or unavailable.

We also recommend that you read the full recipe before you get started in the kitchen.

MEASUREMENTS

Our books are translated and published in several different countries and therefore we always try to adapt our cooking methods, ingredients and measurements so they will work and be easy to follow regardless of where you live. Measurements have sometimes been rounded up or down. Following weights will always give you the most exact result. But if you measure flour in volume, know that a cup should always be full but not packed.

4 cups = 1 litre (34 fl oz)
1 cup = 250 ml (8½ fl oz)
½ cup = 125 ml (4 fl oz)
⅓ cup = 80 ml (3 fl oz)
¼ cup = 60 ml (2 fl oz)
1 tbsp = 15 ml
1 tsp = 5 ml

1 lb = 500 g
2 lb = 1 kg

OVEN SETTINGS

All ovens vary, so you may have to adjust cooking temperatures or times to suit your oven, checking the manufacturer's instructions if possible. The temperatures given in this book are for a conventional oven. If you are using a fan-assisted oven, reduce the temperature by about 20°C (50°F). However, it is important to note that this book uses a fan oven in cases where you're baking with more than one tray at a time – to encourage even baking.

TIME CALCULATIONS

We have given approximate calculations of how long each recipe should take to prepare. We have tried to keep preparation times down so you can spend time with your family while the dinner is cooking. 'Active preparation' is the time you need for chopping ingredients, stirring the pots and making sauces – when you need to be focused on the kitchen. 'Start to finish' is the total time a recipe takes, including inactive cooking time – when your vegetables are in the oven, pasta is cooking or ice cream is in the freezer and you can't use the time to finish another part of the dish. This way you can easily tell that even if it takes 5 days to make our Fizzy Veg (page 162) you only need to spend 15 minutes preparing it.

CHILDREN'S AGES

This book isn't aimed towards a specific age range; our hope is that you use and adapt it regardless of whether you have a two-year-old or a 14-year-old. Maybe blend more food for the younger kids and be more bold with the flavours for older children.

BE CAUTIOUS WITH NUTS

If you have young toddlers or babies you will already know this, but never give them nuts, seeds or large pieces of hard vegetables or fruit as they risk choking on them. If a recipe calls for nuts, make sure to either blend them smooth or leave them out if you are feeding a baby or toddler.

INGREDIENTS

We recommend adapting our recipes to your specific needs. So, feel free to swap in gluten-free and vegan ingredients where necessary – the recipes will be equally delicious. Also, we recommend always using organic produce and dairy products whenever possible.

VEGGIE QUESTIONS

These are topics that you can discuss with your kids. No rights or wrongs, just a method to get them interested in and start thinking more about vegetables and the food they eat. Look for them scattered among the chapter opener pages.

Everyday Meals

How many types of beans do you know?

Do you know any orange vegetables?

Which is your favourite vegetable?

What is the worst vegetable you know, and why?

Weekday Traybake

Serves 4 / Active preparation: 15 minutes / Start to finish: 1 hour

Ingredients

1 kg (2 lb) potatoes, cleaned
    or peeled
4 carrots, tops removed
    and peeled
½ cauliflower head (250 g/9 oz),
    or 1 broccoli head and stalk,
    stalk trimmed
1 garlic bulb, halved
3 tbsp olive oil
sea salt and freshly ground
    black pepper

To serve

½ × 400 g (14 oz) tin black beans,
    rinsed and drained
pesto of choice
torn mozzarella
spiralized courgette (zucchini),
    cucumber, carrot or beetroot
    (beet)
spiralized apple
fresh baby spinach or rocket
    (arugula) leaves
lemon wedges

We can't get enough of traybake dinners in our family. They're simply one of the easiest and most delicious weekday solutions we know. Our trick for keeping it fresh is to mix roasted ingredients with fresh ones and to top it with a good sauce or pesto for a mix of textures and temperatures. Everything is served and arranged directly on the tray. We use a spiralizer to create the vegetable tangles but a julienne peeler also works just fine.

Preheat the oven to 200°C (400°F/gas 6).

Cut the potatoes into wedges, the carrots into bite-size pieces and the cauliflower or broccoli into florets. Transfer the potatoes and carrots to a baking tray (pan), and the cauliflower or broccoli and garlic to a medium-sized bowl. Drizzle all of the vegetables with the oil, season to taste with salt and pepper and toss to coat. Bake the potatoes and carrots for 20 minutes. Remove from the oven, add the cauliflower or broccoli and garlic and bake for a further 25 minutes, or until golden and cooked.

Once cooked, remove from the oven, stir through the beans and serve hot, topped with dollops of pesto, some mozzarella, spiralized veg and apple, spinach or rocket leaves, roasted garlic cloves (squeezed from their peels) and lemon wedges.

 Adult upgrade: *Mix in raw vegetables with the roasted. Spinach, courgettes or cucumber all add different textures to the dish, making it even better. Replace the pesto with Magic green sauce (page 169) for a spicier topping.*

 A helping hand: *Get the kids to clean, scrub or peel the potatoes and carrots. Spiralizing veg and apples is also lots of fun.*

Spinach and Cottage Cheese Waffles

Makes 6 waffles / Active preparation: 20 minutes / Start to finish: 30 minutes

Ingredients

4 eggs, preferably free-range
    and organic
2 bananas, peeled and roughly
    chopped
2 handfuls (50 g/2 oz) of baby
    spinach, roughly chopped
100 g (3½ oz/1 cup) almond flour
125 g (4 oz/½ cup) plain cottage
    cheese
½ tsp baking powder
¼ tsp sea salt
coconut oil or butter

Topping options
(clockwise from top left)

Raspberry and chia jam (page 161),
    crunchy peanut butter, sliced
    banana and desiccated (dried
    shredded) coconut
plain unsweetened Turkish
    or Greek yoghurt, extra virgin
    olive oil and za'atar
PB hummus (page 118), sauerkraut
    and sesame seeds
Chocolate chickpea spread
    (page 167) and toasted sliced
    almonds
smashed avocado, bean sprouts
    and hemp hearts
ricotta, warmed blueberries
    (from frozen) and roughly
    chopped toasted pistachios

The hardest part of making waffles is cleaning the waffle iron afterwards. The rest is a breeze. So bribe someone to do the cleaning part and get going. These spinach-spiked light, fluffy pillows of deliciousness are a balance between sweet and savoury; we show a bunch of different topping suggestions that can take them either way. We usually make a little buffet with topping options to choose from. It might sound fancy but, in practice, it's just a lot of jars from the refrigerator.

Preheat the waffle iron. Crack the eggs into a blender, add the rest of the ingredients (except the oil or butter) and mix until completely smooth.

When the waffle iron is hot, brush with some oil or butter. Pour enough batter onto the waffle iron to completely cover it, close and cook for a few minutes, or until golden. Repeat with the rest of the batter. Serve hot with the topping of your choice.

 Adult upgrade: *Use different toppings as a way to upgrade the waffle to your liking. If you don't like any of the suggestions here, try pulled portobello mushrooms, a muhammara spread or perhaps an aged cheese.*

 A helping hand: *It's easy to burn yourself on the waffle iron so keep younger children at a distance and instead let them help out with making the blender batter. They can also help with placing all the toppings on the table.*

Sushi Burrito Rolls

——— Makes 6 burrito rolls / Active preparation: 30 minutes / Start to finish: 55 minutes ———

Filling

200 g (7 oz/1 cup) wholegrain rice

600 ml (20 fl oz/2½ cups) water

1 sweet potato, peeled

1 tbsp olive oil

1 avocado, stone removed and
    flesh scooped out

150 g (5 oz) red cabbage

1 carrot, top removed and peeled

2 tbsp rice vinegar

1 tbsp maple syrup

sea salt and freshly ground
    black pepper

Ginger mayonnaise

15 g (½ oz) fresh ginger root,
    peeled

80 g (3 oz/⅓ cup) mayonnaise

To assemble

6 nori sheets

toasted black sesame seeds

Do you have half a packet of nori sheets left in the pantry from that one time you made sushi and, because the process was rather fiddly, you haven't got around to making it again? We know the feeling.

This mash-up between sushi and a burrito is simple and fuss-free. The kids love that these are hand-held and portable.

Preheat the oven to 200°C (400°F/gas 6).

To make the filling, bring the rice and water to the boil in a medium-sized lidded saucepan, then reduce the heat and simmer with the lid on for 30 minutes, or until the rice is cooked and most of the water has been absorbed.

Meanwhile, cut the sweet potato into batons, transfer them to a baking tray (pan), drizzle over the oil, season to taste with salt and pepper and toss to coat. Bake for 15 minutes, or until golden and cooked. Slice the avocado and cabbage, cut the carrot into sticks and set aside.

To prepare the ginger mayo, finely grate the ginger, transfer it to a small bowl along with the mayonnaise, stir together and set aside.

Remove the sweet potato from the oven and set aside to cool completely. When the rice is cooked, remove from the heat and set aside for 10 minutes with the lid on, before stirring through the vinegar and maple syrup.

To assemble, place a nori sheet landscape on a sushi mat or clean work surface. Brush the top edge with water and place the bottom edge of another sheet on top so that it forms one long sheet. With wet hands or the back of a spoon (dipped in water), spread a third of the rice out evenly over the sheet on the mat. Top with a third of the sweet potato, avocado, cabbage, carrot and ginger mayonnaise and scatter with sesame seeds. Brush the top edge with water, gently roll the sheet over the filling, tucking it in tightly, and roll up into a log. Repeat with the rest of the sheets and filling. Cut the rolls in half and serve or wrap in parchment paper or reusable food wraps to enjoy later.

 Adult upgrade: *Add wasabi and pickled ginger to your roll if you have that at home.*

 A helping hand: *This is a fun recipe to include the kids. Let them help out with chopping vegetables with a kid-friendly knife, placing them on the nori sheets and rolling the burritos.*

Halloumi Souvlaki Pitta Pockets

——— Makes 6 pitta pockets / Active preparation: 30 minutes / Start to finish: 40 minutes ———

You will need six wooden skewers, soaked in water for 30 minutes

Halloumi souvlaki

1 tbsp dried oregano

1 tbsp dried thyme

1 tbsp dried mint

1 garlic clove, peeled and finely chopped

60 ml (2 fl oz/¼ cup) olive oil

2 tbsp organic apple cider vinegar or red wine vinegar

1 tbsp lemon juice

400 g (14 oz) halloumi (use tofu for a vegan version)

Tzatziki

½ cucumber, peeled and seeds removed

½ courgette (zucchini), topped and tailed

1 tsp sea salt

1 small handful of mint, leaves picked and roughly chopped, or 1 tbsp dried mint

2 garlic cloves, peeled and finely chopped

250 ml (8½ fl oz/1 cup) plain unsweetened Turkish or Greek yoghurt

2 tbsp lemon juice

To serve

6 wholegrain pitta breads, warmed

little gem (bib lettuce) leaves

halved cherry tomatoes

Let's take a quick trip to Greece with these herby-flavoured halloumi skewers. They are super-tasty and have a 'meaty' texture too. Stuff them into pitta bread along with tzatziki, lettuce and tomatoes and you have saved yourself a couple of plane tickets.

Preheat the oven to 220°C (430°F/gas 8) and line a baking tray (pan) with parchment paper.

To make the halloumi souvlaki, grind the dried herbs together in a mortar and pestle, then transfer them to a medium-sized bowl along with the rest of the ingredients, except the halloumi, and stir together.

Cut the halloumi into 2.5 cm (1 in) cubes, add them to the bowl, toss to coat and set aside to marinate.

While the halloumi is marinating, prepare the tzatziki. Coarsely grate the cucumber and courgette, transfer to a sieve (fine mesh strainer), sprinkle with half of the salt and set aside for 10 minutes.

Meanwhile, add the mint to a medium-sized bowl with the garlic and set aside. Rinse and drain the cucumber and courgette, squeeze out any excess water, then transfer them to the bowl along with the rest of the ingredients. Stir together and set aside.

To finish off the halloumi souvlaki, thread three pieces of halloumi onto each skewer, transfer to the prepared tray and drizzle over the marinade from the bowl. Bake for 10 minutes, or until golden and crispy.

Once cooked, remove from the oven and serve hot inside pitta bread pockets filled with some lettuce and tomatoes and topped with dollops of the tzatziki.

 Adult upgrade: *Combine the halloumi with large pieces of red onion, (bell) peppers and mushrooms on the skewers (also covered in marinade) for a more veggie-packed and adaptable recipe. You can also serve this with roasted potatoes as a plated dish. Or skip the pitta bread and simply use the lettuce leaves as a wrap.*

 A helping hand: *Let the kids grind the spices in the mortar and make the tzatziki.*

Middle Eastern Broccoli Tray

Serves 4 / Active preparation: 20 minutes / Start to finish: 30 minutes

Roasted broccoli and chickpeas

2 broccoli heads and stalks
    (500 g/1 lb), trimmed
3 tbsp olive oil
400 g (14 oz) tin chickpeas
    (garbanzos), rinsed and drained
1 tsp ground cinnamon
1 tsp paprika
sea salt, to taste

Tahini yoghurt

125 ml (4 fl oz/½ cup) plain
unsweetened Turkish or
    Greek yoghurt
1 tbsp hulled tahini
1 tsp honey

Cucumber and melon salad

½ cantaloupe melon
    (750 g/1 lb 10 oz), rind and
    seeds removed
4 small Lebanese cucumbers
    or 1 regular cucumber, topped
    and tailed
4 sprigs of mint, leaves only
1 tbsp olive oil
sea salt and freshly ground
    black pepper

To serve

pomegranate seeds
lemon wedges
separated little gem (bib lettuce)
    leaves
wholegrain flatbread triangles

One dish that never fails is a tray of roasted broccoli. There are plenty of ways to mix it up, but this Middle Eastern twist with chickpeas, cinnamon, pomegranate seeds, tahini yoghurt, flatbread and a crunchy melon salad is a recent favourite. We like to eat this with our hands, family style. Everyone grabs a flatbread triangle or lettuce leaf and fills and rolls it up. The kids love it this way, but if you are more of a knife-and-fork kind of person, that of course works as well.

Preheat the oven to 200°C (400°F/gas 6).

To make the roasted broccoli and chickpeas, cut the broccoli into bite-size pieces, transfer them to a baking tray (pan), drizzle with 2 tablespoons of the oil, season with salt and toss. Roast for 10 minutes.

While the broccoli is cooking, put the chickpeas, the rest of the oil and the spices in a small bowl, season to taste with salt and toss to coat. Remove the broccoli from the oven, add the chickpeas and roast for a further 10–15 minutes, or until the broccoli is slightly charred and cooked.

While the broccoli and chickpeas are cooking, prepare the tahini yoghurt. Put all of the ingredients in a small bowl, stir together and set aside.

To make the cucumber and melon salad, cut the melon and cucumber into bite-size pieces and transfer them to a medium-sized serving bowl. Add the rest of the ingredients, season to taste with salt and pepper, stir together and set aside.

When the broccoli and chickpeas are cooked, remove from the oven and serve hot topped with dollops of the tahini yoghurt, a scattering of pomegranate seeds, some lemon wedges, lettuce leaves and flatbread triangles, and with the cucumber and melon salad on the side.

 Adult upgrade: *Serve topped with a sprinkling of za'atar and chilli (hot pepper) flakes.*

 A helping hand: *Let the kids cut the melon and cucumber for the salad. Bonus points for wonky-looking pieces.*

Smash and Tear Summer Pasta

Serves 4 / Active preparation: 20 minutes / Start to finish: 20 minutes

Ingredients

350 g (12 oz) wholegrain
    or bean fettuccine

500 g (1 lb) mixed tomatoes,
    preferably heirloom

2 tbsp capers (baby capers),
    rinsed and drained

1 small handful of basil, leaves only

1 garlic clove, peeled

60 ml (2 fl oz/¼ cup) extra virgin
    olive oil

2 corn cobs, husks removed
    (optional)

sea salt and freshly ground
    black pepper

To serve

2 peaches or nectarines, sliced

200 g (7 oz) torn mozzarella
    or vegan mozzarella

toasted pine nuts or pumpkin
    seeds (pepitas)

basil leaves

extra virgin olive oil

To make this recipe, you need a pair of kid's hands, age 8, to smash the tomatoes into a sauce and tear the mozzarella into chunks. You also need a shirt or dress that can hide any smash-related stains. Seriously, though, this is a super-fun task for the kids and the dish is brilliant in the summer as the sauce isn't heated. Just make sure you use the best tomatoes you can find. We balance out the flavours with sweet peaches, salty capers and charred corn. We also use bean pasta in this recipe; if you prefer using regular pasta, you might want to add some cooked beans for a more balanced dinner. Summer lovin'!

Bring a large saucepan of water to the boil, add a generous sprinkle of salt, followed by the fettuccine and cook according to the packet instructions.

While the fettuccine is cooking, cut the tomatoes in half, crush the capers, tear the basil and finely chop the garlic. Transfer them to a large serving bowl along with the oil, season to taste with salt and pepper and toss together. Smash and squeeze the tomatoes until soft and juicy and set aside for the flavours to enhance.

Meanwhile, preheat a medium-sized griddle pan over a medium-high heat. Chargrill the corn (if using) for a few minutes on each side, or until slightly blackened (or simply add the cobs to the pasta water to cook), then set aside to cool slightly, before cutting the kernels off the cobs.

When the fettuccine is al dente, remove from the heat and drain, reserving half a cup of the cooking water. Add the fettuccine and corn to the bowl with the tomatoes and toss to coat. You may need to add some of the cooking water to loosen the sauce slightly.

Serve warm topped with some peaches and mozzarella, a scattering of pine nuts, some basil and a drizzle of oil.

 Adult upgrade: *Serve topped with a scattering of fresh herbs and a good grind of black pepper.*

 A helping hand: *Smashing and squeezing the tomatoes is a perfect job for the kids. Just make sure they have clean hands and stain-proof clothes.*

Spiralized Root Nests with Eggs

——— *Serves 4–8* / *Active preparation: 25 minutes* / *Start to finish: 45 minutes* ———

Spiralized root nests

750 g (1 lb 10 oz) mixed root
    vegetables (sweet potato,
    beetroot (beet), parsnip, carrot),
    topped, tailed and peeled

2 tbsp olive oil

8 eggs

sea salt, to taste

Cucumber and chickpea salad (adult upgrade)

1 cucumber, topped, tailed
    and peeled

½ × 400 g (14 oz) tin chickpeas
    (garbanzos), rinsed and drained

1 handful of fresh baby spinach

2 tbsp white sesame seeds,
    preferably toasted

2 tbsp lemon juice

1 tbsp toasted sesame oil

sea salt, to taste

Just like a bird's nest, these root nests also carry an egg. Think of them as a modern version of rösti. We make them by simply spiralizing raw roots, dressing them in oil and arranging them on a baking tray (pan). A spiralizer is a fun tool to have in your kitchen as it can transform veggies into new and exciting shapes. However, if you don't have a spiralizer, you can use the coarse side of a box grater instead and just tuck the grated roots into nests. We serve the nests with a cucumber and chickpea salad and a dollop of thick yoghurt on top, but the kids often like to eat them plain. With their hands.

For recipes using two baking trays (pans), a fan-assisted oven gives the most even heat distribution. Preheat fan oven to 180°C (350°F/gas 4) or a conventional oven to 200°C (400°F/gas 6). Grease two baking trays (pans) or line them with parchment paper.

Spiralize the root vegetables, transfer them to a large bowl along with the oil, season to taste with salt and toss to coat. Arrange the root tangles into eight tight nests on the baking trays (pans), making a well in the centre of each one for the eggs. Bake for 25 minutes, or until the vegetables begin to turn golden and crispy. Remove from the oven, carefully crack an egg into the well of each nest and bake for a further 5 minutes, or until the whites have set and the yolks are cooked to your preferred consistency.

While the nests and eggs are cooking, prepare the cucumber and chickpea salad. Slice the cucumber lengthways into ribbons with a mandoline or peeler, transfer them to a medium-sized bowl along with the rest of the ingredients, season to taste with salt, toss together and set aside.

When the nests and eggs are cooked, remove from the oven and serve hot.

 Adult upgrade: *Serve topped with a dollop of yoghurt and a sprinkling of chilli (hot pepper) flakes alongside the cucumber and chickpea salad.*

 A helping hand: *Let the kids spiralize the vegetables. It's a great way to get them playing in the kitchen and, unlike mandolines, spiralizers are pretty safe and difficult to cut yourself on.*

Tofu Cashew Masala

Serves 4 / Active preparation: 20 minutes / Start to finish: 50 minutes

Ingredients

2 tbsp coconut oil

1 onion, peeled and roughly
    chopped

2 garlic cloves, peeled and
    roughly chopped

15 g (½ oz) fresh ginger root,
    peeled and finely grated

1 tsp paprika

1 tsp ground turmeric

1 tsp ground cardamom

½ tsp ground cumin

½ tsp garam masala (optional)

400 g (14 oz) tin chopped
    tomatoes

75 g (2½ oz/½ cup) cashew nuts,
    preferably soaked overnight,
    rinsed and drained*, or 250 ml
    (8½ fl oz/1 cup) double
    (heavy) cream

250 ml (8½ fl oz/1 cup) water
    (omit if using cream)

2 tbsp lemon juice

400 g (14 oz) tofu, patted dry
    and cubed

sea salt and freshly ground
    black pepper

To serve

cooked wholegrain rice

coriander (cilantro) leaves

This is a brilliant little version of an Indian paneer butter masala and it's ever so popular in our home (with one exception – see page 8). It's very simple, rich and flavourful, yet fresh with tons of ginger and lemon. We use tofu instead of paneer and mix cashews into cream instead of using ordinary cream. So it's vegan and allergy-friendly and yet tastes surprisingly much like the original. You can, of course, replace the cashew nuts and water with cream or coconut cream for a more classic version. You can add more vegetables, like broccoli or cauliflower, to the masala if preferred – just add them after the sauce has been mixed.

Heat the oil in a large frying pan (skillet) and sauté the onion, garlic, ginger and spices over a medium-low heat for 15 minutes, or until the onion has softened and the kitchen smells fantastic! Add the tomatoes to the pan, season to taste with salt and a little pepper and simmer for 15 minutes. Remove from the heat, stir through the cashews, water and lemon juice and mix with a hand-held mixer (or heatproof blender) until completely smooth, before returning to the pan.

Add the tofu to the pan and simmer in the sauce for 15 minutes, or until heated through. Serve hot spooned over some rice and topped with coriander.

 Adult upgrade: *Stir in the garam masala after serving the kids. Serve alongside a hefty amount of salad greens to balance out the richness of the sauce.*

 A helping hand: *Let the kids help out with dicing the tofu using a kid-friendly knife, tasting the spices and testing the flavour of the sauce.*

*If you haven't soaked your cashews overnight, cover them with boiling water and set aside for 30 minutes to soak, before rinsing and draining.

Peanut and Sweet Potato Rice Tray

——— Serves 4 / Active preparation: 15 minutes / Start to finish: 1 hour 10 minutes ———

Ingredients

1 sweet potato (250 g/9 oz), peeled
    and roughly chopped

200 g (7 oz) tofu, cubed

1 red onion, peeled and sliced

200 g (7 oz/1 cup) wholegrain rice,
    rinsed and drained

½ x 400 g (14 oz) tin kidney beans,
    rinsed and drained

75 g (2½ oz/1 cup) frozen green beans

15 g (½ oz) fresh ginger root,
    peeled and finely grated

2 garlic cloves, peeled and
    roughly chopped

3 tbsp peanut butter or hulled tahini

2 tbsp tomato purée (paste)

375 ml (12½ oz/1½ cups) good quality
    vegetable stock

250 ml (8½ fl oz/1 cup) coconut milk

sea salt, to taste

To serve

plain unsweetened
    Turkish or Greek yoghurt

roughly chopped toasted peanuts
    or toasted sesame seeds

fresh baby spinach leaves

lime wedges

If you haven't cooked rice on a tray in the oven before, say hello to a new family favourite! This one-tray dinner is simple to make, and tastes rich and sweet with a fresh kick from the ginger, lime and yoghurt. The method can be used for any traditional stew recipe and you'll always end up with the best crispy bits towards the edges of the pan. We often serve this straight from the tray with a couple of forks and glasses on the table. It might seem a bit barbaric but, we promise you, the kids won't complain and neither will the ones doing the dishes.

Preheat the oven to 180°C (350°F/gas 4).

Spread the sweet potato, tofu and onion out in a baking tray (pan) along with the rice, kidney beans and green beans and set aside.

Put the ginger and garlic in a large bowl along with the rest of the ingredients, season to taste with salt and whisk together. Pour over the vegetables and rice and toss together, before spreading everything out evenly, making sure that the sweet potato and rice are submerged in the sauce. Cover with kitchen foil and bake for 45 minutes.

Remove from the oven and discard the foil. Increase the oven temperature to 220°C (430°F/gas 8) and bake for a further 15 minutes, or until the sweet potato and rice are cooked and the sauce forms a crust around the edges of the pan.

Once cooked, remove from the oven, squeeze over one lime and serve hot topped with dollops of yoghurt, a scattering of peanuts and some spinach leaves and extra lime wedges.

 Adult upgrade: *Serve with a salad dressed in a tangy vinaigrette and some chutney on the side.*

 A helping hand: *Let the kids dice the tofu, stir the sauce and toss the rice and vegetables in the sauce. That last bit is pretty messy and fun, so ideal for hooligans who like to get their hands dirty, literally.*

Pick 'n' Mix Salad

Serves 4 / Active preparation: 20 minutes / Start to finish: 30 minutes

Crispy baked green bean fries
300 g (10½ oz) green beans,
    topped and tailed
2 tbsp olive oil
sea salt and freshly ground
    black pepper

Pan-fried tempeh slices
200 g (7 oz) tempeh
1 tbsp olive oil
1 tbsp soy sauce
1 tbsp maple syrup

To serve
cooked millet
corn cobs sprinkled with grated
    Parmesan
sliced cucumber
halved cherry tomatoes
salad greens of choice
sauerkraut or fermented vegetables
    of choice (see Fizzy veg recipe
    page 162)
feta
fresh grapes or seasonal fruit
    of choice
roughly chopped toasted almonds
    or nuts/seeds of choice
Sunny turmeric tahini dressing
    (page 170) or dressing of choice

With kids changing their minds by the hour when deciding which veggies they actually love or hate, this way of eating has saved us many times. We place a number of one-ingredient bowls on the table so that everyone can choose their favourites and build their own salad bowl. This is also a great way to use up any leftovers from earlier in the week. Focus on having a mix of grains, pulses (legumes), fresh vegetables, cheese, fruit, nuts or seeds and one or more dressings and sauces. There are usually one or two cooked 'star ingredients' on the table too, and here it's our simple green bean fries and some fried tempeh. All of the ingredients below are suggestions and interchangeable. Focus on what is in season and what you have at home.

Preheat the oven to 200°C (400°F/gas 6).

Spread the beans out in a baking tray (pan), drizzle over the oil, season to taste with salt and pepper and toss to coat. Bake for 15–20 minutes, or until golden and crispy.

Cook the millet (see page 60 for instructions). Cook the corn cobs in salted water for about 10 minutes.

Slice the tempeh lengthways and place in a shallow bowl. Mix together the oil, soy and maple syrup, pour over the tempeh and marinate for a couple of minutes. Then fry in a pan over medium-high heat for a couple of minutes on each side.

Serve the hot ingredients alongside all of the other salad components and let everyone build their own salad bowl.

 Adult upgrade: *This method is perfect for all ages as you can put some more adult options on the table along with the more kid-friendly ones.*

 A helping hand: *Let your little one count how many bowls are needed and then distribute all the components among them. Older children can also help with frying the tempeh. It's fairly simple to flip the slices; just show them how to hold the pan without burning themselves.*

Tortellini Drop Soup

Serves 4 / Active preparation: 15 minutes / Start to finish: 35 minutes

Ingredients

2 tbsp olive oil

1 onion, peeled and finely chopped

2 garlic cloves, peeled and
finely chopped

2 tbsp tomato purée (paste)

1 tsp paprika

2 carrots (150 g/5 oz), tops removed
and peeled

2 celery stalks (100 g/3½ oz), trimmed
and rinsed

400 g (14 oz) tin chopped tomatoes

1 litre (34 fl oz/4 cups) good-quality
vegetable stock

250 g (9 oz) packet good-quality
fresh tortellini of choice

1 handful of basil, leaves only

sea salt and freshly ground
black pepper

To serve

grated Parmesan

microgreens or sprouts

extra virgin olive oil

A bag of fresh tortellini is a standard weekday rescue dish. But instead of cooking it in water, try cooking it directly in a simple tomato broth or soup. It gives the pasta a lot more flavour and saves on dishes. Our kids love it like this so hopefully yours will too.

Heat the oil in a large lidded saucepan and sauté the onion and garlic with the tomato purée and paprika over a medium-low heat for 5 minutes, or until the onion begins to soften. Cut the carrots and celery into bite-size pieces, add them to the pan and sauté for a further 5 minutes, or until the onion has softened.

Add the tomatoes and stock to the pan, season to taste with salt and pepper and bring to the boil. Reduce the heat and simmer with the lid ajar for 15 minutes, or until the vegetables are cooked.

Add the tortellini to the pan and cook according to the packet instructions, before stirring through the basil.

Serve hot topped with a sprinkling of Parmesan, some microgreens and a drizzle of oil.

 Adult upgrade: *If you're not a fan of tortellini, serve the soup over cooked quinoa and kale instead, or over chickpeas (garbanzos) and burrata/mozzarella.*

 A helping hand: *Let the little ones help by peeling the carrots and chopping the celery into bite-size pieces with a kid-friendly knife. They can be in charge of stirring the broth and finishing the dish with a grating of Parmesan.*

Cauliflower and Tofu Fried Rice

Serves 4 / Active preparation: 25 minutes / Start to finish: 30 minutes

Cauliflower fried rice

200 g (7 oz) tofu, patted dry

2 tbsp coconut oil or ghee

1 red onion, peeled and chopped

1 garlic clove, peeled and chopped

300 g (4 cups/10½ oz) frozen
   vegetable stiry fry mix

125 g (4 oz/2 cups) coarsely
   grated cauliflower

400 g (14 oz/2 cups) cooked
   wholegrain rice*

2 eggs

Marinade

2 tbsp toasted sesame oil

3 tbsp soy sauce or tamari

1 tbsp maple syrup

15 g (½ oz) fresh ginger root,
   peeled and grated

To serve

a handful of cashew nuts,
   finely chopped

lime wedges

*If you haven't precooked your rice,
put 200 g (7 oz/1 cup) wholegrain rice
(preferably soaked overnight, rinsed
and drained) and 625 ml (21 fl oz/
2½ cups) water in a medium-sized
lidded saucepan, bring to the boil,
reduce the heat and simmer with the
lid on for 30 minutes, or until cooked
and most of the water has been
absorbed. Once cooked, remove from
the heat and set aside for 10 minutes
with the lid on, before fluffing up with a
fork and spreading out on a flat dish to
cool completely.

Here is our take on a kids' classic. We have three tricks that make this a winner in our family. First: we grate cauliflower into a rice-like consistency and mix it with the rice for an invisible veg boost (you can go full-cauli and skip the rice entirely but our kids prefer this way). Second: the recipe is based on a packet of frozen stir fry mix. Frozen vegetables have a bad rep but they are actually great – always available, cheap and minimal food waste as you just use what you need and pop the rest back into the freezer. You lose a bit of texture with frozen veg, but cooking speed makes up for it. You can, of course, use a mix of fresh veg in this recipe instead; just fry for them slightly longer. Three: we spruce up the flavours with a great little sweet and salty sauce in which we also marinate the tofu.

Put the marinade ingredients in a medium-sized shallow bowl, stir together and set aside. Cut the tofu into small cubes, add them to the bowl, toss to coat and set aside to marinate.

Heat the oil in a wok pan or large frying pan (skillet) and sauté the onion, garlic and vegetable wok mix over a medium-high heat for 5 minutes, stirring occasionally.

Add the cauliflower to the pan along with the cooked rice and sauté for a further 10 minutes.

Crack the eggs into a small bowl, whisk and pour into a well in the middle of the fried rice. Scramble the eggs and stir through the fried rice along with the tofu and the marinade.

Press a quarter of the fried rice tightly into a small round bowl. Place a serving plate on top of the bowl and carefully turn it upside down, then remove the bowl slowly. Repeat with the rest of the fried rice and top the veggie towers with chopped toasted cashew nuts and lime wedges.

 Adult upgrade: *Add some kimchi or Sriracha to the fried rice.*

 A helping hand: *Let the kids chop the tofu; it is soft and very easy to cut without any accidents. Let them fill the bowls with rice and place them upside down on the plates. Lifting those bowls and revealing the rice dome always brings out oohs and aahs!*

Creamy Broccoli Pasta

Serves 4 / Active preparation: 20 minutes / Start to finish: 30 minutes

Ingredients

350 g (12 oz) lentil pasta or
wholegrain pasta of choice

2 tbsp olive oil

2 broccoli heads and stalks
(500 g/1 lb), trimmed

1 garlic clove, peeled and
finely chopped

1 handful (25 g/1 oz) of fresh spinach,
stems removed and roughly
chopped

250 ml (8½ fl oz/1 cup)
vegetable stock

250 g (9 oz/1 cup) crème fraîche
or vegan cream

1 handful (25 g/1 oz) of basil,
leaves only

2 tbsp lemon juice

sea salt and freshly ground
black pepper

To serve

grated Parmesan

lemon zest

torn basil leaves

Meet our daughter Elsa's favourite pasta dish. She's been eating something similar at school and this is our re-creation after her description. It's funny how much influence kids have on each other. Normally, our boys are a bit hesitant about green sauces but because their big sister says it's good, they like it as well. Another trick is to choose a funny-shaped pasta to take the attention away from the colour of the sauce. This is a red lentil pasta and there are lots of other fun and healthy pasta options popping up in stores these days. If you use regular pasta, you can add some cooked chickpeas (garbanzos) to the pan for a more balanced meal.

Bring a large saucepan of water to the boil, add a generous sprinkle of salt, followed by the pasta and cook according to the packet instructions.

While the pasta is cooking, heat the oil in a large frying pan (skillet) over a medium-low heat. Roughly chop the broccoli (reserving 12 florets to add to the pasta water in the last few minutes of cooking), add to the pan with the garlic and sauté for 5 minutes. Add the spinach and stock, season to taste with salt and pepper, and bring to the boil. Reduce the heat and simmer for 10 minutes, or until the broccoli is cooked. Once cooked, remove from the heat, stir through the crème fraîche, basil and lemon juice, and mix with a hand-held blender until completely smooth.

When the pasta and broccoli florets are al dente, remove from the heat, drain, divide between four bowls and pour the sauce on top.

Serve hot topped with a sprinkling of Parmesan and lemon zest and some torn basil leaves.

 Adult upgrade: *Serve topped with a sprinkling of chilli (hot pepper) flakes alongside a hefty amount of salad greens.*

 A helping hand: *You are the captain and your child is your assistant in this recipe. Read out all the ingredients and let your child guess which drawer or cupboard they can be found in. They can also help with picking florets from the broccoli heads and grating the Parmesan.*

Green Soup with Clouds of Cream

———— Serves 4 / Active preparation: 40 minutes / Start to finish: 45 minutes ————

Spinach and potato soup

2 tbsp olive oil

2 leeks, trimmed, tops removed,
    rinsed and roughly chopped

2 garlic cloves, peeled and
    roughly chopped

8 sprigs of thyme, leaves picked
    and roughly chopped

15 g (½ oz) fresh ginger root,
    peeled and finely grated

600 g (1 lb 5 oz) potatoes, peeled

1 litre (34 fl oz/4 cups) good-quality
    vegetable stock

8 handfuls (200 g/7 oz) of fresh
    spinach, stems removed

sea salt and freshly ground
    black pepper

Magic green beans

200 g (7 oz) green beans, topped,
    tailed and halved

225 g (8 oz/1 cup) Magic green
    sauce (page 169)

To serve

whipped cream or plain
    unsweetened coconut yoghurt

hemp hearts

sliced avocado

extra virgin olive oil

There is a marginal difference between serving a soup with a dash of cream or a dollop of *whipped* cream, but that little detail makes it so much more fun. Especially when you are a kid and the soup is served in cups so it looks like hot chocolate with whipped cream. Except it isn't hot chocolate, it's a potato and leek soup with spinach that tastes really good and not as green as it looks. The flavours are pretty simple, which is exactly what many kids like about it. However, for adults we recommend going all-in with flavourful and textural toppings for contrast.

Heat the oil in a large lidded saucepan and sauté the leeks, garlic, thyme and ginger over a medium-low heat for 5 minutes, or until the leeks begin to soften. Cut the potatoes into bite-size pieces, add them to the pan and sauté for a further 10 minutes, or until the leeks have softened. Add the stock, season to taste with salt and pepper and bring to the boil. Reduce the heat and simmer with the lid ajar for 15 minutes, or until the potatoes are cooked.

While the soup is cooking, prepare the magic green beans. Bring a small saucepan of water to the boil, add the beans and blanch for a couple of minutes, or until al dente. When ready, remove from the heat, drain, toss to coat in the magic green sauce and set aside.

When the soup is ready, remove from the heat, stir through the spinach and mix with a hand-held blender until completely smooth.

Serve hot topped with the magic green beans, a dollop of cream, a scattering of hemp hearts, some avocado and a drizzle of oil.

 Adult upgrade: *The magic green beans and avocado topping are the upgrade in this recipe. Kids usually like it simple and smooth, whereas adults appreciate the textures and flavours that the toppings add.*

 A helping hand: *Let the kids help out with peeling the potatoes, mixing the soup (with your help) and, of course, whipping the cream.*

Carrot and Ginger Patties with Creamy Potatoes

Serves 4 / Active preparation: 45 minutes / Start to finish: 45 minutes

Carrot and ginger patties

1 egg

500 g (1 lb) carrots, tops removed, peeled and finely grated

15 g (½ oz) fresh ginger root, peeled and finely grated

8 sprigs of dill, fronds picked and finely chopped

75 g (2½ oz/¾ cup) rolled oats

½ tsp sea salt

olive oil, for frying

Creamy potato salad

500g (1 lb) baby potatoes, washed

1 tsp coarse sea salt

4 eggs

8 sprigs of dill, fronds picked and roughly chopped (adult upgrade)

250 ml (8½ fl oz/1 cup) plain unsweetened Turkish or Greek yoghurt

200 g (7 oz) cucumber, topped and tailed

8 black olives, pitted and roughly chopped

2 tbsp capers (baby capers), rinsed and drained

sea salt and freshly ground black pepper

These carrot patties are usually a pretty safe card with kids. Sweet and easy to make, they can be eaten inside a burger bun, and they are good both warm and cold. The creamy potato salad is the perfect side dish.

To make the carrot and ginger patties, crack the egg into a large bowl and whisk. Add the carrots, ginger, dill, oats and salt to the bowl and mix together. Form into a ball in the bowl and set aside for at least 15 minutes for the mixture to 'glue' together.

Meanwhile, prepare the creamy potato salad. Cut the potatoes into bite-size pieces and cover with water in a medium-sized saucepan. Add the salt and bring to the boil, then reduce the heat and gently boil for 10 minutes, or until cooked.

Put the eggs into a small saucepan, cover with water and bring to the boil, then reduce the heat and gently boil for 10 minutes.

While the potatoes and eggs are cooking, mix together the dill and yoghurt in a large bowl, and season to taste with salt and pepper. Cut the cucumber in half lengthways before thinly slicing and adding to the bowl along with the olives and capers.

When the potatoes and eggs are cooked, remove from the heat, drain and set aside to cool completely. Peel the eggs, cut into quarters and add to the bowl along with the potatoes. Gently toss together and set aside.

To finish off the carrot and ginger patties, heat a little oil in a large non-stick frying pan (skillet) over a medium-high heat. Form the mixture into 8 patties and transfer to the pan. Fry for a few minutes, or until golden underneath. Carefully flip each patty with a spatula and fry on the other side for a further few minutes, or until golden.

Serve hot alongside the creamy potato salad.

 Adult upgrade: *Dill and ginger can be an acquired taste. If your kids don't like them, divide the salad in two parts and add the dill to the adult half.*

 A helping hand: *Grating carrots is the perfect task for kids; a box grater is easy to handle and fairly safe. If you are worried that they will cut themselves, tell them to grate only half the carrot and then you can do the rest. Another fun assignment is to form the carrot patties.*

Tommy Pepper Soup

——— Serves 4 / Active preparation: 30 minutes / Start to finish: 40 minutes ———

Ingredients

2 tbsp olive oil

500 g (1 lb) carrots, tops removed,
    peeled and coarsely grated

1 onion, peeled and chopped

5 sprigs of thyme, leaves picked
    and chopped

200 g (7 oz/1 cup) jarred roasted
    red (bell) peppers, drained and
    roughly chopped

400 g (14 oz) tin chopped tomatoes

125 g (4 oz/½ cup) red lentils,
    preferably soaked overnight, rinsed
    and drained

1 litre (34 fl oz/4 cups) good-quality
    vegetable stock

2 tbsp lemon juice

sea salt and freshly ground
    black pepper

Sourdough stars

1 tbsp olive oil

4 slices of sourdough rye
    or gluten-free bread

To serve

plain unsweetened Turkish or
    Greek yoghurt

extra virgin olive oil

This tip-top tomato, (bell) pepper and lentil soup comes together in half an hour and you only need a handful of essentials (if you don't think a jar of roasted peppers is a pantry essential, this soup is here to change that). Spend five extra minutes making our star-shaped sourdough rye bread croûtons and little yoghurt starry sky to start dinner with a smile. This soup also tastes great chilled and is perfect in a jar to take to the park.

To make the soup, heat the oil in a large lidded saucepan and sauté the carrots, onion and thyme over a medium-low heat for 5 minutes, or until the onion begins to soften. Add the peppers to the pan and sauté for a further 5 minutes, or until the onion has softened. Add the tomatoes, lentils and stock, season to taste with salt and pepper and bring to the boil. Reduce the heat and simmer with the lid ajar for 15–20 minutes, or until the lentils are cooked.

While the soup is cooking, prepare the sourdough stars. Use a mini star (or heart) cookie cutter to cut stars out of the bread (any leftover bits can be roughly chopped and toasted as regular croûtons for less fussy adults). Heat the oil in a large frying pan (skillet) and fry the stars over a medium heat for a few minutes on each side, or until golden, and set aside.

When the soup is cooked, remove from the heat, stir through the lemon juice and mix with a hand-held blender until completely smooth. Serve hot dotted with yoghurt (using the back of a teaspoon) and topped with the sourdough stars and a drizzle of oil.

 Adult upgrade: *Stir a sprinkling of paprika or chilli powder through the yoghurt before spooning it over the soup, and serve topped with some leafy greens and sesame seeds that have been sautéed in olive oil and drizzled with lemon juice.*

 A helping hand: *Cutting out the croûtons and decorating the soup is a task tailor-made for kids.*

Pumpkin and Chocolate Stew with Millet

Serves 6 / Active preparation: 30 minutes / Start to finish: 50 minutes

Ingredients

200 g (7 oz/1 cup) millet

500 ml (17 fl oz/2 cups) water

1 tsp sea salt

2 tbsp raisins

2 tbsp olive oil, coconut oil or ghee

2 onions, peeled and finely chopped

1 tbsp tomato paste (purée)

2 garlic cloves, finely chopped

1 tsp paprika

1 tsp dried oregano

1 pumpkin (900 g/2 lb)
   or carrots, peeled diced

400 g (14 oz) tin chopped tomatoes

400 g (14 oz) tin white beans,
   drained and rinsed

30 g (1 oz) dark chocolate (at least
   70% cocoa solids)

1 large handful of coriander (cilantro)
   or parsley, to serve (adult upgrade)

sea salt and freshly ground
   black pepper

This stew is the perfect vegetarian dish for all ages. The pumpkin has a sweet flavour and soft texture, but what we usually sell it on is the fact that it contains chocolate!

Dry-roast the millet in a medium-sized saucepan over a low heat for 2–3 minutes, then add the water and salt, increase the heat and bring to the boil. Reduce the heat and simmer for about 8–9 minutes. Remove from the heat and leave to sit for a few minutes to absorb all the water. Use a fork to fluff up the millet and mix in the raisins.

   Heat the oil in another pan and add the onions, tomato paste and garlic. Sauté until translucent, then add the paprika and oregano, stirring to prevent the spices from burning. Add the pumpkin, tomatoes and 500 ml (17 fl oz/ 2 cups) water and bring to a simmer. Cook for about 30 minutes, or until the pumpkin is tender. Season to taste with salt and pepper. Stir in the beans and chocolate. Taste and adjust the flavours to your liking. Serve with the cooked millet.

 Adult upgrade: *We think this dish needs a big pile of fresh herbs stirred through but our kids don't agree, so the solution is to keep the herbs on the side and add to your own dish.*

 A helping hand: *Let the kids help by fluffing up the millet with a fork and adding the raisins. They can also help out with rinsing the beans, stirring the pan, and they will definitely want to add the chocolate!*

Courgette Carbonara with 'Parsnip Pancetta'

———— Serves 4 / Active preparation: 25 minutes / Start to finish: 25 minutes ————

Ingredients

200 g (7 oz) wholegrain spaghetti

2 parsnips, tops removed and peeled

4 tbsp olive oil

1 red onion, peeled and thinly sliced

2 garlic cloves, peeled and
    finely chopped

1 courgette (zucchini), topped
    and tailed

100 g (3½ oz/½ cup) sour cream

2 egg yolks

2 tbsp grated Parmesan

2 tsp lemon zest

sea salt and freshly ground
    black pepper

To serve

grated Parmesan

extra virgin olive oil

4 sprigs of flat-leaf parsley (optional)

Spaghetti carbonara must be one of the most popular kids' dishes of all time. No wonder; it's plain and creamy with lots of spaghetti and crispy chunks of something salty-sweet. In our version we use small chunks of parsnip that crisp up just like pancetta, and we mix spiralized courgettes into the spaghetti to amp up the vegetable content. but still with a similar flavour and texture to the original.

Bring a large saucepan of water to the boil, add a generous sprinkle of salt, followed by the spaghetti and cook according to the packet instructions.

While the spaghetti is cooking, cut the parsnips into small batons. Heat half of the oil in a large frying pan (skillet) and sauté the parsnips and onion with a pinch of salt over a medium-low heat for 10 minutes, or until the onion begins to soften. Add the garlic to the pan along with the remaining oil and sauté for a further 5 minutes, or until the onion has caramelised and the parsnips are golden and crispy.

While the vegetables are cooking, spiralize the courgette and set aside. Put the sour cream, egg yolks, Parmesan and lemon zest in a medium-sized bowl. Season to taste with salt and pepper, whisk together and set aside.

When the spaghetti is al dente, remove from the heat and drain, reserving a cup of the cooking water.

Add the spaghetti to the frying pan along with a splash of the cooking water, the sour cream mixture and the courgettes and quickly but gently toss together. The heat from the spaghetti will delicately cook the yolks just enough to thicken into a smooth and silky sauce and not scramble. You may need to add more of the cooking water to loosen the sauce slightly.

Serve straight away topped with a sprinkling of Parmesan, a drizzle of oil and a sprig of parsley, if you like.

 Adult upgrade: *Amp up the freshly ground black pepper, stir through chopped parsley and serve alongside a hefty amount of salad greens.*

 A helping hand: *Spiralizing the courgettes is a fun process that the kids will love to be in charge of.*

Portobello and Avocado Quesadillas

Serves 4 / Active preparation: 20 minutes / Start to finish: 20 minutes

Ingredients

150 g (5 oz) portobello mushrooms

2 tbsp coconut or olive oil

2 tsp soy sauce

2 tsp maple syrup

1 tsp apple cider vinegar

2 avocados, stone removed
 and flesh scooped out

½ × 400 g (14 oz) tin black
 beans, rinsed and drained

8 tortillas

1 lime, quartered

1 handful of parsley, leaves picked
 and finely chopped (optional)

100 g (3½ oz/½ cup) grated Cheddar

4 tbsp plain unsweetened Turkish or
 Greek yoghurt

sea salt

These cheese-and-mushroom-packed little triangles are our way of doing fast food at home. Eaten with our hands, from a tray on the living-room rug in front of a movie, they are the essence of comfort. We fill them with sweet and sticky mushrooms, mashed avocado, cheese, beans and a layer of yoghurt to lighten them up.

Clean and slice the mushrooms and chop the stems. Heat the oil in a frying pan (skillet) and add the mushrooms. Fry for a couple of minutes on each side, then add the soy sauce, maple syrup and vinegar and season with salt. Fry for another couple of minutes. Transfer to a plate and wipe the pan clean.

Mash the avocado flesh and beans separately with a fork and set aside. Heat the frying pan without any oil and add one tortilla. Spread a quarter of the avocado mash over it and scatter over a quarter of the mashed beans and half of the mushroom slices. Squeeze over some lime juice and scatter with parsley (if using) and cheese. Spread a thin layer of yoghurt over another tortilla and place it on top, yoghurt-side down. Carefully flip the whole tortilla and fry it on the other side for a couple of minutes until the cheese has melted. Slide it off to a cutting board and cut into smaller wedges. Repeat with the remaining ingredients and serve immediately.

 Adult upgrade: *Make a standard quesadilla for the kids but add pickled jalapeños or a good grind of black pepper to the second. Serve with Magic green sauce (page 169) or another sauce drizzled over.*

 A helping hand: *A child can easily chop the mushrooms, especially since they end up hidden inside the tortilla so they don't need to look pretty. They can also help by mashing the avocado and beans with a fork.*

Rainbow Pancakes

———— Makes 10–14 pancakes / Active preparation: 25 minutes / Start to finish: 45 minutes ————

Ingredients

5 eggs

150 g (5 oz/1 cup) rice (or spelt) flour

500 ml (17 fl oz/2 cups) oat milk

½ tsp sea salt

2 tbsp butter or coconut oil, for frying

Rainbow vegetable add-ins (choose one of these)

1 large handful of spinach + 1 small handful of herbs (basil, mint or parsley)

1 raw beetroot (beet), peeled and grated

1 raw carrot, peeled and grated

To serve

cottage cheese

carrots, grated

lemon juice

When we asked our readers which of our recipes they make most often for their children, the response was the pancakes from our book *Green Kitchen at Home*. It's also one of the most popular recipes in our home. So, at the risk of repeating ourselves, we felt like we couldn't release this book without including them. It's just such a simple way to eat, appreciated by both kids and adults and boosted with extra vegetables.

Crack the eggs into a blender or food processor. Add the flour, milk, salt and the vegetable add-in of choice and mix on high speed until smooth. Leave to rest for 20 minutes before frying the pancakes (you can fry them right away but they will be a little harder to flip).

For frying, add a little butter or coconut oil to a 20 cm (8 in) non-stick frying pan (skillet) over a medium heat. Once hot (this is important or else the pancakes will stick), whisk the batter then ladle 80 ml (2¾ fl oz/⅓ cup) into the pan. Fry for 1–2 minutes, or until small bubbles form on the surface and the base is golden. Run a spatula around the edges to make sure the pancake has detached from the pan, before carefully flipping it over and frying the other side for another minute. Transfer to a plate and repeat with the rest of the batter (you may need to reduce the heat slightly after the first pancakes).

If not using straight away, you can store the pancakes in an airtight wrap in the refrigerator and they will be good for 3–4 days. You can also store the batter in a closed container in the refrigerator for 2–3 days. Serve rolled up with cottage cheese and grated carrots with a squeeze of lemon juice in the middle.

 Adult upgrade: *Serve the pancakes rolled up with crumbled feta, sauerkraut and a basil and kale salad with a lemon vinaigrette inside.*

 A helping hand: *Let the kids help make the batter. Older kids can also help by pouring the batter into the pan and even flipping the pancakes, but it is a little fiddly and younger children risk burning themselves so they are better off adding whatever toppings you want to serve them with. See page 129 to see how to make spinach and banana pancake rolls.*

Roasted Veg Blender Soup with Halloumi Croûtons

Serves 4 / Active preparation: 20 minutes / Start to finish: 45 minutes

Ingredients

1 kg (2 lb) mixed cauliflower, carrot
    and pumpkin in equal amounts,
    trimmed and peeled

1 onion, peeled and quartered

2 garlic cloves, peeled and smashed

2 tbsp olive oil

1 tsp sea salt

1 tsp ground cinnamon

½ tsp ground cumin

750 ml (25 fl oz/3 cups) vegetable
    stock

60–125 ml (2–4 fl oz/¼–½ cup) plant
    based milk

1 tbsp apple cider vinegar

Halloumi croûtons

1 tsp olive oil

200 g (7 oz) halloumi, cubed

If you haven't made roasted vegetable soup, this is your roll call. By roasting the vegetables you'll get all those caramelised/charred bits that carry more flavour and add greater depth. It's also easier because you don't need to be in the kitchen stirring the pot. Simply roast all the veggies in a roasting pan on high heat in the oven and then add them to your blender with the rest of the ingredients. It's a great way to finish up any odd bits and bobs that are hiding in the refrigerator, so it doesn't have to be equal amounts of the vegetables – go with what you've got.

The halloumi croûtons are ideal as a soup topping as the heat from the soup will keep them soft and squidgy.

Preheat the oven to 200°C (400°F/gas 6) and line a baking tray (pan) with baking parchment.

Cut the mixed veg into large bits and place on the baking tray (pan) along with the onion and garlic. Drizzle with the olive oil and sprinkle with the salt, cinnamon and cumin. Toss so that everything is covered in oil and spices. Roast for about 30 minutes, or until slightly charred.

Meanwhile, heat the vegetable stock in a saucepan. If your blender is approved for hot liquids, transfer the roasted vegetables to it, pour over the stock and blend until smooth (always make sure the lid is secured when blending hot liquids). You can also simply place the vegetables in the saucepan with the stock and use a hand-held blender to mix until smooth. Add the milk to make it creamier and apple cider vinegar to give it a slight tang. Taste and add more milk, water or spices if needed.

Continued overleaf

To make the halloumi croûtons, add the oil to a non-stick frying pan (skillet) and fry the halloumi cubes over a medium heat for a 1–2 minutes on each side.

Serve the soup with the croûtons on the side. See the adult upgrade for instructions on how to make kale chips.

Adult upgrade: *Make kale chips to go with the soup. Simply tear a couple of kale leaves into smaller pieces and discard the thick stems. Toss in a little olive oil, salt and ground cinnamon (or chilli powder) and spread out on a baking tray (pan). Place in the oven as you remove the vegetables. Reduce the heat to 160°C (320°F/gas 2) and bake for 10–15 minutes until the edges are brown but not burnt.*

A helping hand: *Let your little ones help with chopping the halloumi into squares (or whatever they turn into). If you have swimming goggles at home, you can also demonstrate how to chop an onion while looking funny and without shedding a tear.*

Rye Gözleme with Corn and Avocado Dip

———— Serves 4 / Active preparation: 30 minutes / Start to finish: 30 minutes ————

Flatbread

150 g (5 oz/1 ½ cups) light rye flour

120 g (5 oz/½ cup) cultured
buttermilk or plain unsweetened
Turkish or Greek yoghurt

½ tsp baking powder

½ tsp sea salt

Filling

2 tbsp olive oil

120 (5 oz/¾ cup) sweet corn kernels
from a tin (or 2 fresh corn on the
cob with kernels shucked off),
rinsed

2 handfuls of baby spinach leaves

150 g (5 oz/1 cup) feta, crumbled

Avocado dip

2 avocados, stone removed and flesh
scooped out

juice of 1 lime

2 tbsp water

a pinch sea salt

This is a Scandinavian take on a Turkish flatbread where we use a cultured buttermilk and rye flour to create a tangy and wholesome bread that can be ready within minutes. It's fried in a pan and folded over a simple corn, spinach and feta filling that melts inside. You can replace the corn with black beans to make the filling even more nourishing and use any tangy yoghurt instead of buttermilk.

Add half the flour to a medium-sized bowl along with all of the buttermilk, the baking powder and sea salt. Use a wooden spoon to stir the ingredients into a dough, sprinkling over a handful more flour as you go. Use your hands to make it come together into a ball that can be shaped easily. If it feels too sticky, simply sprinkle with a little extra flour. Divide the ball into four equally sized pieces. Put a cloth over the bowl and let the dough rest while preparing the filling.

Add half of the oil to a large frying pan (skillet) over a medium heat. Add the corn and let it get some colour for a few minutes before adding the spinach. When the spinach has wilted, scoop it into a bowl and crumble over two-thirds of the feta. Clean out the pan with a paper towel.

Add the remaining feta to a food processor along with the avocado, lime juice, water and salt. Mix until smooth, then scoop into a small bowl.

Sprinkle your surface with the remaining flour and flatten out the dough balls into medium-thin discs using your fingers or a floured rolling pin. Heat the frying pan until medium hot and brush it with olive oil. Place two of the flatbreads and add to the pan, add the filling and immediately fold them into half moons. Give the edges a light squeeze with a spatula to close them. Let fry on one side for about two minutes, or until charred, then carefully flip them and fry for another minute, brushing the bread with extra oil if they look dry. Repeat with the remaining two flatbreads.

Cut each flatbread into triangles and serve with avocado dip and a side salad.

 Adult upgrade: *Chop a green chilli finely and add to the filling of your portions. Serve with a salad or a cabbage slaw on the side.*

 A helping hand: *Making the flatbread dough is an easy job so let your kids add the ingredients and work them into a ball.*

Watermelon and Halloumi Salad Bowls

—— Serves 4 / Active preparation: 25 minutes / Start to finish: 25 minutes ——

Ingredients

1 watermelon (about 3 kg/6 lb 10 oz), halved

1 tbsp olive oil

200 g (7 oz) halloumi or vegan halloumi, cubed

100 g (3½ oz) mixed cherry tomatoes, preferably heirloom, halved

400 g (14 oz) tin chickpeas (garbanzos), rinsed and drained

2 handfuls of mâche (lamb's lettuce) or salad greens of choice

8 sprigs of mint, leaves only

3 tbsp extra virgin olive oil

2 tbsp lime juice

sea salt, to taste

To serve

toasted pumpkin seeds (pepitas)

lime wedges

This is one of our family's favourite summer dishes. It's super-fresh and the watermelon balances the salty halloumi just perfectly. It looks fun served inside a watermelon 'bowl', but you can, of course, just use a regular serving dish. We simply flavour the salad with lime, mint and olive oil for the kids and then upgrade it with an herby sauce for ourselves.

Run a knife around the inside of the watermelon halves, 1 cm (½ in) or so away from the rind. Cut the flesh into segments, scoop them out and set aside, reserving the hollowed-out halves to use later as serving bowls.

Heat the oil in a medium-sized saucepan and fry the halloumi over a medium-high heat for a few minutes on each side, or until golden.

While the halloumi is cooking, cut the watermelon flesh into cubes and transfer to a large bowl with the tomatoes. Set aside.

When the halloumi is cooked, remove from the heat and add to the bowl along with rest of the ingredients. Toss together.

Serve straight away inside the watermelon bowls, topped with a scattering of pumpkin seeds (pepitas) and some lime wedges.

 Adult upgrade: *Serve topped with a generous drizzle of Magic green sauce (page 169).*

 A helping hand: *Let the kids help with scooping out the watermelon flesh with a spoon. It will keep them occupied while you have time to prep the other steps.*

Stuffed Sweet Potato Boats

—— Serves 4 ——

Let your kids prepare this easy and comforting recipe for dinner.
It is as effortless as it is tasty.

1. Ingredients: 2 large sweet potatoes, 250 g (9 oz/1 cup) plain unsweetened Turkish or Greek yoghurt, 165 g (6 oz/1 cup) cooked chickpeas (garbanzos), 1 tbsp lemon juice, 2 tsp curry powder, 1 tsp salt, 4 tbsp pumpkin seeds (pepitas), 2 tsp olive oil, 4 tbsp shredded cheese, a handful of pomegranate seeds

2. Place the sweet potatoes on a baking tray (pan) in the oven and set it to 200°C (400°F/gas 6). Let them bake for about 50 minutes or until the can easily be pierced with a fork. Use oven mittens when removing the baking tray (pan). Note: Time may vary depending on size.

3. Let the sweet potatoes cool off a bit, then cut them in half and scoop out the flesh, leaving a little flesh towards the edges to hold their shape.

4. Place the flesh in a bowl along with yoghurt, chickpeas (garbanzos), lemon juice, curry and salt.

5. Use a fork to mix it all up.

6. Brush the sweet potato boats with oil, add the filling and top with the pumpkin seeds (pepitas) and cheese. Place back into the oven for 15-20 minutes until the cheese has melted an started to get a little colour. Top with pomegranate seeds.

Party Food

What can you make with chickpeas (garbanzos)?

Which vegetables grow where you live?

Name five vegetables in five different colours?

Which is the prettiest vegetable you know?

Stuffed Rainbow Tomatoes

——— Serves 6–8 / Active preparation: 30 minutes / Start to finish: 1 hour 10 minutes ———

Ingredients

200 g (7 oz/1 cup) red or black rice

500 ml (17 fl oz/2 cups) vegetable
stock or water

½ tsp sea salt

1.5 kg (3 lb 5 oz) mixed tomatoes
with stems, preferably heirloom

300 g (10½ oz/2 cups) feta
or tofu, crumbled

½ × 400 g (14 oz) tin black beans,
rinsed and drained

75 g (2½ oz/½ cup) raisins

2 tsp ground cinnamon

olive oil, to brush

To serve

plain unsweetened Turkish or
Greek yoghurt

roughly chopped mint leaves

We've been making this recipe for years and have been simplifying it every time. This is the easiest version we have ever made and it's also the most flavoursome. We save the tomato pulp and seeds and add them directly to the boiling rice, which gives it a fabulous flavour. It's a real show-off of a recipe when using heirloom tomatoes but regular tomatoes work fine as well.

Preheat the oven to 200°C (400°F/gas 6) and grease a baking tray (pan) or line it with baking parchment.

Put the rice, stock and salt in a medium-sized lidded saucepan, bring to the boil, then reduce the heat and simmer with the lid on for 30 minutes, or until cooked and most of the water has been absorbed.

While the rice is cooking, cut off and reserve the caps from the tomatoes and cut out and discard the hard white core. Scoop out the pulp and seeds, add them to the pan of simmering rice and transfer the tomatoes to the tray, cut-side up, along with the caps. When the rice is cooked, remove from the heat and set aside for 10 minutes with the lid on, before fluffing up with a fork. Add the rest of the ingredients, except the oil, to the pan and stir together.

Fill up the tomatoes with the stuffing, top them with the caps and brush with the oil. Bake for 15 minutes, or until the tomatoes are lightly browned and cooked. Once cooked, remove from the oven and to with a dollop of yoghurt and some fresh mint. Serve immediately.

 Adult upgrade: *Serve alongside a hefty amount of salad greens.*

 A helping hand: *Let the little ones scoop out the tomato pulp and seeds with a teaspoon and also help with stuffing the tomatoes with rice.*

Family Veggie Hotpot

Serves 4 / Active preparation: 30 minutes / Start to finish: 40 minutes

Marinated tofu

60 ml (2 fl oz/¼ cup) soy sauce
    or tamari

2 tbsp toasted sesame oil

2 tbsp maple syrup

1 tsp lime zest

300 g (10½ oz) tofu, patted dry

Miso broth

1 tbsp coconut oil

2 spring onions (scallions), trimmed,
    tops removed and thinly sliced

30 g (1 oz) fresh ginger root, peeled
    and thinly sliced

4 tbsp white miso paste

2 litres (70 fl oz/8 cups) good-quality
    vegetable stock

For dunking

quartered brown button mushrooms

carrot ribbons

sliced pak choi (bok choi)

baby corn

mung bean sprouts

sugar snap peas

cooked rice or soba noodles drizzled
    with toasted sesame oil

To serve

toasted peanuts

coriander (cilantro) leaves

medium-boiled egg halves (optional)

cubed watermelon

lime wedges

Luise and I grew up in the 1980s when the fondue pot was an obligatory part of a kitchen. I remember loving the ceremony of sitting together around a pot of hot oil, dipping meat or veggie skewers into it. We make a similar but yet very different dish with our kids today. Instead of oil, we have a large pot of heated miso broth that we dunk vegetables, tofu and noodles into, and then serve with toasted peanuts, fresh coriander, a squeeze of lime juice, medium-boiled eggs and watermelon. It's fun and delicious and the best part is that the kids get to arrange their own bowls, so no sour faces. All of the vegetables in this recipe are suggestions so feel free to adapt it with what you can find. A tip is to stick to vegetables that can be eaten raw or barely blanched. The longer the broth cooks with all the veggies in it, the more flavourful it will become.

To make the marinated tofu, put all of the ingredients, except the tofu, in a medium-sized bowl and stir together. Wrap a paper towel around the tofu and firmly but carefully press out as much liquid as possible. Then cut the tofu into slices 2 cm (¾ in) thick, transfer them to the bowl, toss to coat and set aside to marinate.

While the tofu is marinating, prepare the miso broth. Heat the oil in a large saucepan or fondue pot and sauté the spring onions and ginger over a medium-low heat for 10 minutes, or until the spring onions begin to soften. Add the miso paste and sauté for a further 5 minutes, or until the spring onions have softened. Add the stock to the pan, bring to the boil, then reduce the heat and simmer for 15 minutes.

Arrange all the ingredients on the table and let everyone build their own bowls by dunking the vegetables, tofu and noodles into the simmering broth and fishing them out along with some broth.

Serve hot topped with a scattering of peanuts, some coriander, eggs (if using) and watermelon, and a squeeze of lime juice.

 Adult upgrade: *Serve topped with a drizzle of chilli oil and some kimchi to create more heat.*

 A helping hand: *This recipe is fun for kids to help out with. Put all the dipping ingredients on the table and let them be in charge of placing them in different bowls while you get some peace and quiet to prepare the broth.*

Baked Coconut Tempura Veggies

Serves 4–6 / Active preparation: 50 minutes / Start to finish: 1 hour

Sticky rice balls

200 g (7 oz/1 cup) Thai black rice,
   preferably soaked overnight,
   rinsed and drained
625 ml (21 fl oz/2½ cups) water
2 tsp toasted sesame oil
2 tsp rice vinegar
2 tsp soy sauce or tamari

Tempura veggies

250 g (9 oz) butternut squash,
   rind and seeds removed
½ cauliflower head (250 g/9 oz)
200 g (7 oz) mushrooms
   of choice, cleaned
1 avocado (150 g/5 oz),
   stone removed and flesh
   scooped out
100 g (3½ oz) tofu, patted dry

Coconut tempura batter

2 eggs, or 125 ml (4 fl oz/½ cup)
   aquafaba
125 g (4 oz/1 cup) almond flour
100 g (3½ oz/1 cup) desiccated
   (dried shredded) coconut
½ tsp sea salt
¼ tsp freshly ground black pepper

Dipping vegetables in a batter and baking until golden and crispy is a simple trick to make them more fun and accessible for kids. Our method is easier and healthier than any deep-fried version and the almond flour and desiccated (dried shredded) coconut add a pleasant sweetness and crunch. We serve these on a large platter with our sticky rice balls, dipping sauce and various other raw veggies and fruit. Aquafaba is simply the liquid from a tin of chickpeas (garbanzos).

Preheat the oven to 180°C (350°F/gas 4) and grease a baking tray (pan) or line it with baking parchment.

To make the sticky rice balls, bring the rice and water to the boil in a medium-sized lidded saucepan, then reduce the heat and simmer with the lid on for 30 minutes, or until cooked and most of the water has been absorbed. While the rice is cooking, prepare the veg: cut the squash into slices 1 cm (½ in) thick, the cauliflower into florets, the mushrooms into halves or quarters, the avocado into wedges, the tofu into bite-size triangles, and set aside.

To make the coconut tempura batter, crack the eggs into a medium-sized bowl and whisk together. Put the rest of the ingredients in a separate medium-sized bowl and stir together. Dip the vegetables in the egg mixture, before tossing in the coconut mixture and transferring to the prepared tray. Bake for 15–25 minutes, or until the vegetables are cooked, golden and slightly crispy. Remember to turn the vegetables over halfway through the cooking time.

Continued overleaf

Dipping sauce

60 ml (2 fl oz/¼ cup) soy sauce
   or tamari

2 tbsp toasted sesame oil

2 tbsp rice vinegar

½ tsp white sesame seeds,
   preferably toasted

To serve

red cabbage leaves

avocado wedges

sugar snap peas

pea tendrils

pineapple triangles

lime wedges

While the vegetables are cooking, make the dipping sauce. Put all of the ingredients, except the sesame seeds, in a small serving bowl and stir together. Scatter with the sesame seeds and transfer to a serving platter.

When the rice is cooked, remove from the heat and set aside for 10 minutes with the lid on, before stirring through the oil, vinegar and soy sauce. Mash the rice with a fork until it is sticky. Working with one heaped tablespoon of rice at a time, roll into balls and transfer to a serving platter.

When the vegetables are cooked, remove from the oven, transfer to the platter and serve hot alongside the sticky rice balls, some cabbage, avocado, sugar snap peas, pea tendrils, pineapple and lime wedges, and with the dipping sauce on the side.

 Adult upgrade: *Serve with Sriracha sauce.*

 A helping hand: *Set up work stations and let your child/children dunk the veggies in the egg mixture and the coconut.*

Rye Empanadas with Mushrooms and Raisins

——— Makes 30 empanadas / Active preparation: 1 hour / Start to finish: 1 hour 10 minutes ———

Filling

2 tbsp olive oil

1 red onion, peeled and
    finely chopped

2 garlic cloves, peeled and
    finely chopped

250 g (9 oz) brown button
    mushrooms, cleaned and
    roughly chopped

1 tsp dried thyme

250 g (9 oz) carrots, tops removed,
    peeled and coarsely grated

75 g (2½ oz/½ cup) walnuts, roughly
    chopped (optional)

400 g (14 oz) tin black beans,
    rinsed and drained

100 g (3½ oz/1 cup) grated cheese
    of choice (optional)

3 tbsp raisins

sea salt, to taste

Dough

500 g (1 lb/4 cups) plain (all-purpose)
    flour, sifted, plus extra for dusting

225 g (8 oz/2 cups) rye flour, sifted

250 g (9 oz) unsalted butter,
    cubed and chilled

1 tsp sea salt

2 eggs

250 ml (8½ fl oz/1 cup) water
    or milk of choice, chilled

Egg wash

1 egg

1 tbsp water

To be honest, this is a bit of a weekend project, but it pays off on days when you're out of time and energy and have hungry kids shouting in your ears. Simply grab a few empanadas from the freezer, shove them in the oven and you'll soon feel pretty good about yourself again. We tend to prepare a big batch, then freeze half of them unbaked and bake and eat the rest during the week. They also make great finger food at a party. Let the kids help out with making them – chopping the mushrooms, cutting out the dough, filling the empanadas and sealing the edges with a fork are all good tasks for little hands.

Preheat the oven to 200°C (400°F/gas 6) and grease a baking tray (pan) or line it with baking parchment.

To make the filling, heat the oil in a large frying pan (skillet) and sauté the onion and garlic over a medium-low heat for 5 minutes, or until the onion begins to soften. Add the mushrooms to the pan along with the thyme and sauté for a further 5 minutes. Next add the carrots, walnuts (if using), and beans. Season to taste with salt and sauté for a further 5 minutes. Once cooked, remove from the heat and set aside to cool slightly, before stirring through the cheese (if using) and raisins.

To prepare the dough, put the flours, butter and salt in a food processor and pulse until the mixture resembles fine breadcrumbs. Crack the eggs into the food processor, add half of the water and pulse until the mixture comes together to form a dough. You may need to add the some or all of the rest of the water. Transfer to a floured work surface and knead the dough slightly to bring it together to form a ball. Cut the ball in half; cover one half with a clean tea (dish) towel and roll out the other half so that it is 5 mm (¼ in) thick. Using a 12.5 cm (5 in) round cookie cutter or small bowl, cut out as many circles as you can before rolling out the remaining dough and repeating so that you have 15 circles in total. Repeat with the other half of the dough.

Continued overleaf

To make the egg wash, crack the egg into a small bowl, add the water, whisk together and set aside.

To assemble, place a couple of tablespoons of the filling in the middle of each dough circle. Brush the edges with the egg wash. Gently pull the edge of the circle away from the work surface, fold it over the filling and seal and crimp the edges with your fingers or a fork. Repeat with the rest of the circles and filling.

Freeze half of the empanadas (if you like); transfer the rest to the prepared baking tray (pan) and brush with the remaining egg wash. Bake for 25 minutes, or until golden and crunchy. Once cooked, remove from the oven and serve hot with your favourite dipping sauce, pesto or yoghurt.

 Adult upgrade: *Serve with some Magic green sauce (page 169) for dipping and a leafy green salad. You could also make spicier empanadas with pickled jalapeños and rice added to the stuffing.*

 A helping hand: *Let the kids chop the mushrooms (they are hidden inside the empanadas so quirky bits are allowed), and help with cutting out the dough, filling the empanadas and sealing the edges with a fork.*

Dino Burgers

Makes 6–8 mini burgers / Active preparation: 40 minutes / Start to finish: 1 hour

Spinach and pea patties

100 g (3½ oz/½ cup) black quinoa, rinsed and drained

250 ml (8½ fl oz/1 cup) water

3 handfuls (75 g/2½ oz) of fresh spinach, stems removed and roughly chopped

300 g (10½ oz/2 cups) frozen peas, thawed

2 sprigs of basil, stems removed

2 eggs, preferably free-range and organic

75 g (2½ oz/¾ cup) (gluten-free) rolled oats

50 g (2 oz/½ cup) grated pecorino or Parmesan

2 tbsp lemon juice

1 tsp sea salt

olive oil, for frying

Burger dressing

5 tbsp mayonnaise

2 tbsp capers (baby capers), rinsed, drained and chopped

1 tbsp good-quality ketchup

To assemble

mini sourdough or gluten-free buns

good-quality ketchup

sliced tomatoes

crispy lettuce leaves

We often tell stories about how strong the food we eat makes us. Take these burgers, for instance. They're packed with spinach and quinoa and we all know that Popeye loves spinach and he's the strongest person ever! It's also obvious that dinosaurs devoured quinoa. You can tell just by looking at their skin – it looks like the texture of quinoa, doesn't it? Need more proof? Just try these delicious burgers and you'll see for yourself. You'll be as strong as a sailor and as tall as a dinosaur. Who knows, you might even be able to breathe fire like a dragon. That's what good food does to you.

To make the spinach and pea patties, bring the quinoa and water to the boil in a small lidded saucepan, then reduce the heat and simmer with the lid on for 15 minutes, or until small tails appear and the water has been absorbed.

While the quinoa is cooking, put the spinach in a food processor with the peas and basil and blend until almost smooth. Crack the eggs into a large bowl and whisk. Add the pea mixture to the bowl along with the rest of the ingredients, except the oil. When the quinoa is cooked, fluff up with a fork and set aside to cool. Add the quinoa to the bowl and mix together. Form into a ball in the bowl and set aside for at least 15 minutes for the mixture to 'glue' together.

Meanwhile, prepare the burger dressing. Put all of the ingredients into a small bowl, stir until combined and set aside.

Form the spinach and pea mixture into 8 patties, about 100 g (3½ oz) each, and fry in a little oil in a large non-stick frying pan (skillet) over a medium-high heat for a few minutes, or until golden underneath. Carefully flip each patty with a spatula and fry on the other side for a further few minutes, or until golden.

To assemble, cut the buns in half, spread the bottom half with the burger dressing and the top half with ketchup. Put a patty on top of each bottom bun, top with tomato slices, lettuce and the top bun and serve hot.

 Adult upgrade: *Add mashed avocado and more veggie toppings to the burgers. Or serve the patties over salad and grains in a bowl instead.*

 A helping hand: *Get the kids to help out with forming the patties. Preparing and slicing the 'assembly' ingredients and arranging them on a large platter will also be a fun job for them.*

Butternut Börek Snake

Serves 6–8 / Active preparation: 1 hour / Start to finish: 1 hour 30 minutes

Filling

2 tbsp olive oil

2 onions, peeled and finely chopped

2 garlic cloves, peeled and
  finely chopped

1 tsp dried oregano

1 butternut squash
  (about 750 g/1 lb 10 oz),
  rind and seeds removed

½ tsp ground cinnamon

4 handfuls (100 g/3½ oz) of fresh
  spinach or Swiss chard, stems
  removed

1 small handful of flat-leaf parsley,
  stems removed

2 tbsp lemon juice

300 g (10½ oz/2 cups) feta,
  crumbled

sea salt and freshly ground
  black pepper

Egg wash

2 eggs

125 ml (4 fl oz/½ cup) plain
  unsweetened Turkish or
  Greek yoghurt

4 tbsp olive oil or melted butter
  (or 125 ml/4 fl oz/½ cup if
  omitting eggs and yoghurt
  for a vegan version)

One of our kids' favourite takeaway treats are börek hand pies from the Turkish corner shop close to where we live. They are normally not crazy about chard, but when it's paired with feta and wrapped in a thin and crusty filo dough (or yufka) crust, they devour it. So that's how we like to use filo pastry – as a magic wrapping paper in which we can put basically any vegetable along with a little bit of cheese and get our kids' approval.

Börek cigars are easy to make but if you want to turn it into a party dish, you can attach the cigars to each other and bend and fold a bit to make it look like a snake lurking in the green salad 'grass'.

Preheat the oven to 200°C (400°F/gas 6) and grease a baking tray (pan) or line it with baking parchment.

To make the filling, heat the oil in a large lidded frying pan (skillet) and sauté the onions, garlic and oregano over a medium-low heat for 5 minutes, or until the onions begin to soften. Cut the squash into bite-size pieces and add to the pan along with the cinnamon, season to taste with salt and pepper and sauté for a further 25 minutes with the lid on, or until the squash is cooked but still holds its shape. Stir occasionally to prevent the onions and garlic from burning. While the squash is cooking, roughly chop the spinach and parsley and set aside. When the squash is cooked, remove from the heat, stir through the spinach, parsley and lemon juice and set aside to cool slightly, before stirring through the feta.

To prepare the egg wash, crack the eggs into a medium-sized bowl, add the rest of the ingredients, whisk together and set aside.

To assemble, place two filo dough sheets landscape on top of each other on a clean work surface. Brush the top sheet with the egg wash and spread a quarter of the filling out evenly in a line at the bottom of the sheet. Gently pull the edge of the sheet away from the work surface, roll it over the filling, tucking it in firmly, and roll up tightly into a log. Repeat with the rest of the sheets (bar one) and the filling.

Continued overleaf

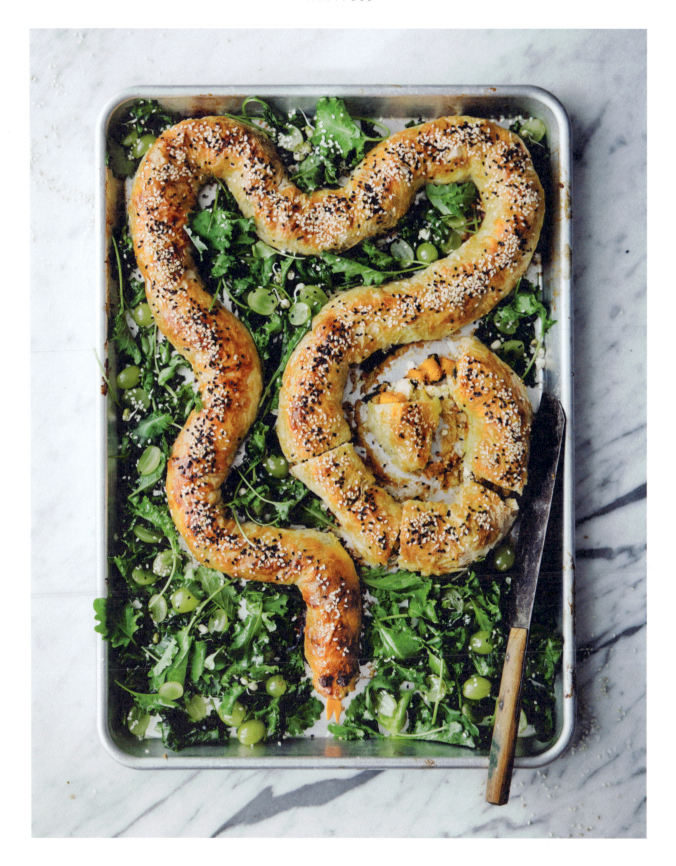

To assemble

9 sheets (gluten-free) filo dough
    or yufka

black and white sesame seeds
    or nigella seeds

To serve

raisins

carrot ribbon

mâche (lamb's lettuce)

mung bean sprouts

halved green grapes

Transfer to the prepared baking tray (pan), join the ends of the logs together and form into the shape of a coiled snake. Tear the last sheet of filo dough into strips and wrap around the ends of the logs to cover the intersections (you can also use this method to easily patch up the snake if the filling leaks out somewhere. Once baked, any patchwork will be invisible).

Brush the snake with the egg wash and sprinkle with sesame seeds. Bake for 30 minutes, or until golden and crispy.

Once cooked, remove from the oven and place two small raisins as eyes and a carrot ribbon as a tongue on the snake's head.

Once the tray has cooled down, cover with some mâche, mung bean sprouts, grape halves and sesame seeds to create the 'grass' around the snake. Serve warm alongside some 'grass' salad.

 Adult upgrade: *Add some ground cumin, chilli (hot pepper) flakes and more spinach to the filling and serve over a salad bowl with pickled vegetables.*

 A helping hand: *Kids can help with making the egg wash and brushing the pastry. They can also lend a hand with shaping and building the snake and be in charge of making the salad grass.*

Jewelled Quinoa Salad

—————— Serves 4 / Active preparation: 30 minutes / Start to finish: 45 minutes ——————

Ingredients

3 tbsp olive oil

60 ml (2 fl oz/¼ cup) lemon juice

2 tsp ground cinnamon

½ tsp ground cardamom

¼ tsp ground cumin

1 butternut squash
   (about 750 g/1 lb 10 oz),
   rind and seeds removed

200 g (7oz/1 cup) white quinoa,
   rinsed and drained

500 ml (17 fl oz/2 cups) water

1 orange, peeled

½ handful (12 g/½ oz) of mint
   leaves

½ × 400 g (14 oz) tin chickpeas
   (garbanzos), rinsed and drained

40 g (1½ oz/⅓ cup) raisins

3 tbsp extra virgin olive oil

sea salt and freshly ground
   black pepper

To serve

a handful of toasted almonds,
   chopped

a handful of pomegranate seeds

This salad is based on our very popular Moroccan quinoa salad recipe, featured in our book *Green Kitchen Travels*. We have turned it into a more child-friendly version with lots of sweet and fresh flavours and small colourful pieces of fruit and vegetables (looking like jewels). We serve this salad in jars with spoons, which for some reason makes it feel less like a salad. It also turns it into a good little dish to serve at a kids' party.

Preheat the oven to 200°C (400°F/gas 6).

Put the olive oil, half the lemon juice, half the cinnamon and the cardamom and cumin in a large bowl, season to taste with salt and pepper, stir together and set aside.

Cut the squash into small bite-size pieces and add to the bowl, tossing to coat. Transfer to a baking tray (pan) and bake for 30 minutes, or until golden and cooked.

While the squash is cooking, bring the quinoa, water and the rest of the cinnamon to the boil in a medium-sized lidded saucepan, then reduce the heat and simmer with the lid on for 15 minutes, or until small tails appear and the water has been absorbed.

While the quinoa is cooking, segment and cut the orange into bite-size pieces, roughly chop the mint and set aside. When the quinoa is cooked, remove from the heat and fluff up with a fork, before spreading out on a dish to cool slightly.

When the squash is cooked, remove from the heat and add to the dish with the quinoa, along with the orange pieces, mint, the remaining lemon juice and the rest of the ingredients. Season to taste with salt and pepper and toss together.

Spoon into four glasses, jars or bowls and serve topped with a scattering of almonds and pomegranate seeds.

 Adult upgrade: *This salad is amazing served inside baked aubergine (eggplant) halves and drizzled with tahini.*

 A helping hand: *Let the kids mix together the butternut squash marinade and then toss the prepped squash in it. They can also help by picking the seeds from the pomegrante and by spooning the salad into glasses or jars.*

Dips, Chips and Sticks

Each spread makes 300 g (10½ oz/2 cups) / Active preparation: 30 minutes / Start to finish: 30 minutes

Herby hummus

1 handful of fresh spinach,

400 g (14 oz) tin chickpeas
  (garbanzos), rinsed and drained

4 tbsp hulled tahini

1 garlic clove, peeled

3 sprigs of flat-leaf parsley,
  stems removed

2 sprigs of mint, stems removed

4 tbsp lukewarm water

2 tbsp extra virgin olive oil (optional)

2–3 tbsp lemon juice

½ tsp sea salt

Muhammara spread

200 g (7 oz/1 cup) jarred roasted
  red (bell) peppers, drained

75 g (2½ oz/½ cup) walnuts or
  sunflower seeds, preferably toasted

65 g (2¼ oz/½ cup) almond flour

1 soft date, pitted

2 tbsp extra virgin olive oil

1 tbsp lemon juice

½ tsp sea salt

¼ tsp ground cumin

Salted yoghurt

2 sprigs of flat-leaf parsley or
  coriander (cilantro), stems removed

500 ml (17 fl oz/2 cups) plain
  unsweetened Turkish or
  Greek yoghurt

4 tbsp extra virgin olive oil

4 tbsp lime juice

1–2 tsp sea salt

Here are three dips/spreads to try out for your next movie night. We serve these with a mix of veggie sticks and root vegetable crisps (chips) that the kids absolutely love. This together makes more than you need for one night, but they are also great as sides for dinner or inside a sandwich or wrap.

For the herby hummus roughly chop the spinach, transfer it to a food processor along with the rest of the ingredients and blend until your desired consistency is achieved. Taste and adjust the flavours. Store in an airtight jar or container in the refrigerator for up to 5 days.

For the muhammara spread roughly chop the peppers, transfer them to a food processor along with the rest of the ingredients and blend until your desired consistency is achieved. Taste and adjust the flavours. Store in an airtight jar or container in the refrigerator for up to 5 days.

For the salted yoghurt finely chop the parsley, transfer it to a small bowl along with the rest of the ingredients and stir together. Taste and adjust the flavours. Store in an airtight jar or container in the refrigerator for up to 5 days.

To serve

extra virgin olive oil

roughly chopped toasted almonds or sunflower seeds

mixed root vegetable chips

carrot sticks

celery sticks

cucumber sticks

quartered radishes

Serve topped with a drizzle of oil and a scattering of almonds (for the muhammara spread) alongside the chips and crudités.

 A helping hand: *Get the little ones to prepare the serving ingredients and arrange all the different elements on a serving platter.*

Potato, Courgette and Feta Pizza on a Cauliflower Base

———— *Makes 1 large pizza / Active preparation: 40 minutes / Start to finish: 1 hour 10 minutes* ————

Ingredients

1 large (500 g/ 1 lb) cauliflower head

100 g (4 oz/1 cup) almond flour

1 tsp dried oregano

1 tsp sea salt and freshly ground
    black pepper

4 eggs

Potato topping

3 medium-sized firm potatoes

1 small courgette (zucchini)

2 tbsp sea salt

4 tbsp olive oil

100 g (3½ oz/¾ cup) feta, crumbled

1 small red onion, peeled
    and thinly sliced

2 tbsp thyme leaves,
    roughly chopped

sea salt and freshly ground
    black pepper

Adult upgrade

4 tbsp Magic green sauce (page 169)
    or pesto

baby kale or rocket (arugula)

lemon juice

We often talk about pizza as a vessel that we can pile with lots of vegetables and get our kids to eat happily. But if we are to be entirely honest, they usually scooch most of the toppings off, only to be left with little margherita pieces (plain tomato sauce and cheese). Potato pizza is always a hit with our kids, though. Crunchy, carby and without too many weird textures on top. Our favourite thing about it is that it's so simple. We make it pizza bianca-style, so no sauce needed. We are serving it on a cauliflower base here, which is another smart little veg-boosting trick (the almond flour gives it a sweet flavour). But for an even easier version, you can use Lebanese flatbreads as a base and then it's ready in no time. Even if we keep it simple for the kids, we add extra greens to our pieces so everyone ends up happy.

Preheat the oven to 200°C (400°F/gas 6) and line a baking tray (pan) with parchment paper.

To make the cauliflower base, coarsely chop the cauliflower (use the brighter part of the stem too), place in a food processor and blend until you have a fine rice-like texture. Measure 1 litre (34 fl oz/4 cups) of the vegetable 'rice' and place in a mixing bowl. Add the almond flour, oregano, salt and pepper and mix with your hands. Make a well in the middle and add the eggs. Whisk the eggs with a fork. Use your hands to pull the dry ingredients towards the middle until everything is combined and you can shape it into a ball. It should be more loose and wet than a traditional bread dough. Leave to sit for 10 minutes. Transfer to the prepared baking tray (pan) and shape into a large pizza by flattening the dough with your hands, making the edges slightly higher. Bake in the middle of the oven for 15 minutes, or until slightly golden and firm.

Continued overleaf

Meanwhile, prepare the potato topping. Slice the potatoes and courgette very thinly with a mandoline or a knife. Place the slices in a deep plate, sprinkle them with the salt and cover with cold water for 20 minutes. Drain the water, rinse and pat the potatoes and courgette dry on a tea (dish) towel.

Brush the baked cauliflower base with a thin layer of the olive oil. Cover it with half of the feta, then add the potato and courgette slices, onion, thyme and, finally, the remaining feta. Season with salt and black pepper. Drizzle with more of the olive oil and bake for about 15 minutes until the potatoes are golden and the edges are slightly burnt.
Serve immediately.

 Adult upgrade: *Top the baked pizza with a drizzling of Magic green sauce (page 169) and some baby kale dressed in lemon juice.*

 A helping hand: *A pizza doesn't have to be round or square, it can look however you want it to. So let the children be in charge of shaping the pizzas. Show how they should flatten out the dough and let them decide whether to make one large or several smaller shapes. Let them also put topping on their own pizza slice.*

All-in-one Lasagne

——— Serves 4-6 / Active preparation: 30 minutes / Start to finish: 1 hour 15 minutes ———

Tomato sauce

3 tbsp olive oil

2 onions, peeled and finely chopped

3 garlic cloves, peeled and
finely chopped

2 tbsp tomato purée (paste)

2 tbsp capers (baby capers)

3 × 400 g (14 oz) tins
chopped tomatoes

250 g (9 oz) white cabbage

2 handfuls of basil, leaves picked
and roughly chopped

75 g (2½ oz/½ cup) cooked puy lentils

250 g (9 oz/1 cup) crème fraîche

sea salt

Lasagne elements

250 g (9 oz) wholegrain
lasagne sheets

grated cheese of choice

Lasagne usually has two or three different sauces and always feels like a rather big project to start. This is a quick all-in-one version where you stir down lentils, cabbage and crème fraîche into the tomato sauce before layering with lasagne sheets. It saves on dishes and still tastes fantastic. When white cabbage is heated, it develops a texture and look similar to lasagne sheets and slips down invisibly with the kids.

Preheat the oven to 200°C (400°F/gas 6).

To make the tomato sauce, heat the oil in a large saucepan and sauté the onions, garlic, tomato purée and capers over a medium heat, stirring, for a couple of minutes. Add the tomatoes, rinsing out the tins with a little extra water to stir through the sauce. Season with salt and simmer for 20 minutes.

Discard the thick stem from the cabbage and roughly chop the leaves. Add to the sauce along with the basil and simmer for 5 minutes, then fold in the lentils and crème fraîche and take off the heat.

Scoop a thin layer of the tomato sauce into the bottom of a 20 × 30 cm (8 × 12 in) baking tray (pan). Add a layer of lasagne sheets, then a layer of tomato sauce and a sprinkling of grated cheese. Continue with lasagne sheets and repeat the layers until you run out of sheets and sauce. There should be a final layer of sauce with cheese on top.

Place in the oven and bake for 30–40 minutes, or until the lasagne is golden and the sheets are soft.

 Adult upgrade: *Prepare a large salad with a lemon vinaigrette to serve with the lasagne.*

 A helping hand: *Let your child/children add the lasagne sheets for each layer. It's kind of like a puzzle, arranging the noodles to cover the layers, and nobody will taste if they don't fit perfectly.*

 Tip: *If you want a slightly lighter and fresher version, you can replace half of the crème fraîche with yoghurt.*

Cucumber Sailing Boats

— Serves 4 —

A deconstructed salad in the shape of a sailboat is a fun and simple concept to serve children vegetables at a party. Scraping out cucumber halves, filling them with cheese and making vegetable sails is also a great way to keep kids of all ages occupied preparing it, so you have time to focus on other tasks. We are using cream cheese, but goat's cheese or feta would also work. Or even hummus for a vegan option.

1. Measure out the ingredients: 1 cucumber (cut into 4 pieces), 2 yellow (bell) peppers, 8 black olives, 8 cherry tomatoes, 120 g (5 oz/½ cup) cream cheese, toothpicks or wooden skewers.

2. Divide the cucumbers in half lengthwise and use a small spoon to scrape out the seeds.

3. Cut off a thin strip of the back of each cucumber to make the boats more stable.

4. Fill the cucumber halves with cream cheese.

5. Cut the (bell) pepper vertically along the sides where the rounded parts of it intersect, giving you natiral looking sails.

6. Place a tomato and olive on a toothpick and use it as the mast for the sailboat, skewering it through the (bell) pepper and into the cucumber, holding everything together.

Lunchbox Favourites

Which is the ugliest vegetable you know?

Lentils can have different colours – how many colours do you know?

Which fruits and vegetables would you put in your dream salad?

How many colours have you eaten today?

Lunchbox Beet Spread Buns

Makes 250 g (9 oz/1 cup) / Active preparation: 10 minutes / Start to finish: 30 minutes

Ingredients

2 beetroots (beets) (200 g/7 oz),
    tops removed and peeled
    (or precooked)

2 sprigs of dill, stems removed
    and roughly chopped

40 g (1½ oz/¼ cup) sunflower seeds,
    preferably soaked overnight,
    rinsed and drained

125 ml (4 fl oz/½ cup) plain
    unsweetened Turkish or
    Greek yoghurt

2 tbsp lemon juice

¼ tsp sea salt

To assemble

mini sourdough or gluten-free buns

salted butter of choice

Other lunchbox items

carrot sticks

sliced cucumber

Orange bliss balls (page 151)

quartered apples

Dried apple rings (page 143)

Our kids are obsessed with anything mini-sized and these sourdough buns are no exception. The beet spread is sweet and crunchy with tangy tones from the yoghurt and lemon, suiting the soft buns perfectly. We often buy precooked vacuum-sealed beetroots for this but have included cooking instructions if you prefer cooking them yourself.

Cut the beetroot into bite-size pieces, transfer them to a medium-sized saucepan, cover with water and bring to the boil. Reduce the heat and gently boil for 20 minutes, or until cooked. Once cooked, remove from the heat, drain and set aside to cool completely. Add the dill to a food processor along with the beetroot and the rest of the ingredients and blend until your desired consistency is achieved.

Store in an airtight jar or container in the refrigerator for up to 5 days. To assemble, cut buns in half, spread the bottom half with the beet spread and the top half with butter. Put the buns back together, wrap in parchment paper or reusable food wraps, and pack in a lunchbox along with the selection of lunchbox items.

 A helping hand: *Let your child spread the beet spread over their own sandwich.*

Omelette Rolls with Broccoli Pesto

———— Active preparation: 15 minutes / Start to finish: 25 minutes ————

Broccoli pesto

Makes 300 g (10½ oz/1½ cups)

1 broccoli head and soft part of stalk
    (250 g/9 oz), trimmed

75 g (2½ oz/½ cup) cashew nuts
    or sunflower seeds, preferably
    toasted

1 handful (25 g/1 oz) of basil

2 tbsp raisins

60 ml (2 fl oz/¼ cup) extra
    virgin olive oil

60 ml (2 fl oz/¼ cup) lemon juice

½ tsp sea salt

Omelette

Makes 1 omelette

1 tbsp olive oil or butter

1 egg

1 tbsp milk of choice

¼ tsp sea salt

To assemble

sliced avocado

Other lunchbox items

scored avocado halves with a squeeze
    of lemon juice

cream cheese-stuffed red peppers

carrot sticks

Fizzy veg (cauliflower florets)
    (page 162)

drained tinned corn kernels

pitted soft dates

One-egg omelettes are quick and easy to make and are a great snack or lunchbox food. Roll them up with this broccoli pesto, which we've slightly sweetened with raisins, and creamy avocado slices and you have a nutritious lunch done in no time. You could replace the avocado with cheese sticks, if you like. This pesto also makes a great spread, dip and sauce stirred through pasta or quinoa.

To make the broccoli pesto, place a steaming basket (or simply a metal sieve (fine mesh strainer) or colander) inside a large saucepan and bring about 5 cm (2 in) water to the boil. Roughly chop the broccoli, transfer it to the basket and steam for a few minutes, or until al dente. Once al dente, remove from the heat and set aside to cool completely.

Put the broccoli in a food processor along with the rest of the ingredients and blend until your desired consistency is achieved. Store in an airtight jar or container in the refrigerator for up to 5 days.

To prepare the omelette, put the oil in a medium-sized non-stick frying pan (skillet) over a medium-high heat. Crack the egg into a small bowl, add the rest of the ingredients and whisk together. Pour the egg mixture into the pan and cook for a minute, or until golden underneath and almost set on top. Carefully flip with a spatula and cook on the other side for a further 15 seconds, or until golden.

Once cooked, remove from the heat and set aside to cool completely. To assemble, spread the omelette with the broccoli pesto and top with avocado slices. Roll the omelette up, cut in half, wrap in parchment paper or reusable food wraps, and pack in a lunchbox along with the other items.

 A helping hand: *A child can help by adding the pesto ingredients to the food processor and pulsing them to the desired consistency. Ask if they like the pesto chunky or smooth.*

PB Hummus and Carrot Flatbread Rolls

Makes 350 g (12 oz/1½ cups) hummus / Active preparation: 15 minutes / Start to finish: 15 minutes

Peanut butter hummus

400 g (14 oz) tin chickpeas
   (garbanzos), rinsed and drained
4 tbsp smooth peanut butter or
   hulled tahini
3 tbsp hot water
1 garlic clove, peeled
2 tbsp lemon juice
½ tsp sea salt
1 tsp ground cinnamon
¼ tsp ground cumin

To assemble

wholegrain or gluten-free flatbreads
coarsely grated carrot
crispy lettuce leaves

Other lunchbox items

grapes
halved baby cucumbers
sauerkraut

Hummus with peanut butter instead of tahini is a popular alternative with many kids, as it tastes richer and nuttier. Spread it on flatbread with grated carrot and crispy lettuce leaves on top, roll the flatbread up and slice it into sandwich rolls. This makes more hummus than you need for the flatbread rolls, but simply store the leftovers in an airtight container in the refrigerator.

Put all of the hummus ingredients in a food processor and blend on high speed. Taste and add more water or lemon juice if needed. Mix again until your desired consistency and flavour is achieved.

Store in an airtight jar or container in the refrigerator for up to 5 days. To assemble, spread the flatbreads with the peanut butter hummus and top with grated carrot and lettuce leaves. Roll the flatbread up, cut into pieces, wrap in parchment paper or reusable food wraps, and pack in a lunchbox along with the lunchbox other items.

 A helping hand: *In this recipe, a child can help out with measuring and adding the peanut butter and squeezing the lemon juice. Let them taste the hummus and ask if they think it's good or if it needs anything else. This will help them feel that it is their hummus.*

Oat and Courgette Pang Cakes

Makes 10 small pancakes / Active preparation: 10 minutes / Start to finish: 15 minutes

Ingredients

2 eggs

1 banana, peeled and
    roughly chopped

100 g (3½ oz/1 cup) rolled oats

2 tbsp milk of choice

½ tsp sea salt

¼ tsp baking powder

½ courgette (zucchini) (100 g/3½ oz),
    top removed and coarsely grated

coconut oil or butter, for frying

Other lunchbox items

sliced yellow (bell) peppers

cherry tomato skewers

sliced pears

dried apricots (preferably without
    sulphur dioxide)

cashew nuts

'PANG CAKES!' is our son's most common answer when asked what to put in his lunchbox for his Friday forest hike with preschool. He means small, thick American-style pancakes, and because they're on repeat, we try to mix up the recipe for variation. We often make the spinach pancakes from our *Green Kitchen at Home* book. Unlike that one, this version has courgette grated through but the best thing is how simple they are, with oats as the only grain. They literally take five minutes to prep and five minutes to fry, so totally do-able even on a stressful morning.

Crack the eggs into a blender. Add the banana along with the rest of the ingredients, except the courgette and oil, and mix until completely smooth. Stir the courgette through the batter with a spoon.

Heat a little oil in a large non-stick frying pan (skillet) over a medium-high heat. Pour a few tablespoons of the batter for each pancake into the pan and fry for a minute, or until golden underneath and small bubbles appear on the surface. Carefully flip each pancake with a spatula and fry on the other side for a further minute, or until golden. Repeat with the rest of the batter. Once cooked, remove from the heat and set aside to cool completely.

Wrap in parchment paper or reusable food wraps, and pack in a lunchbox along with the other items.

 A helping hand: *Let the kids grate the courgette on the box grater. If you feel comfortable letting your kids handle a frying pan, they can also flip the pancakes (supervised, of course!). The first ones are always a little wobbly but after that they are quite firm and easily flippable.*

Pasta Salad with OJ Pesto

Makes 185 g (6½ oz/¾ cup) pesto / Active preparation: 10 minutes / Start to finish: 15 minutes

OJ and basil pesto

3 tbsp orange juice

4 tbsp olive oil

1 large handful of basil

2 tbsp capers (baby capers), drained

10 almonds or cashew nuts

pinch of sea salt

Pasta salad

10–15 green beans, topped and tailed

100 g (3½ oz/1 cup) cooked pasta
    of choice

4 heirloom tomatoes, halved

Other lunchbox items

1 medium boiled egg, preferably
    free-range and organic, halved

3 dates tossed, in cacao powder

2 tbsp fermented red cabbage
    sauerkraut

This is a slightly sweeter version of pesto with orange juice instead of lemon and cashew nuts to give it that nice rich flavour. It's a good thing to try if your kids are suspicious of ordinary pesto. Also, if you let them make their own pesto, chances are about 500 per cent higher that they will like it. So let them take the lead on this.

Mix the pesto ingredients in a food processor or grind them in a pestle and mortar until smooth. Steam the beans until tender (you could do this in a sieve (fine mesh strainer) over the pan as you cook the pasta, or even add them to the water towards the end of the cooking time). Mix the pesto in with the cooled pasta. Combine the tomatoes and beans with the pasta. Add to a lunchbox and with the other items.

 A helping hand: *Pesto is such an easy, adaptable recipe, so let the kids pour in the ingredients and hit the mixing button (with a little supervision, of course) until it has the consistency and flavour they like.*

Crispy Rice Paper Rolls

—————— Makes 10 rice paper rolls / Active preparation: 15 minutes / Start to finish: 35 minutes ——————

Filling

2 carrots (250 g/9 oz), tops
    removed and peeled
75 g (2½ oz / ½ cup) frozen peas
75 g (2½ oz/½ cup) crumbled feta
1 tsp lemon juice
sea salt and freshly ground
    black pepper

Egg wash

1 egg
1 tbsp plain unsweetened yoghurt
    (optional)
1 tbsp olive oil
¼ tsp sea salt

To assemble

5 rice paper sheets
nigella seeds

Other lunchbox items

lacto-fermented cucumber
banana halves
cherry tomatoes on a stick
dark chocolate-covered rice cakes

You can use rice paper for more than just fresh summer rolls. We like to add a filling to them, brush them with oil and yoghurt and bake them into easy crispy rolls. The kids love these little parcels and they pack well in a lunchbox. Here we keep the filling super-simple but anything goes, so let your imagination run wild!

Preheat the oven to 200°C (400°F/gas 6) and grease a baking tray (pan) or line it with baking parchment.

To make the filling, coarsely grate the carrots and transfer them to a large bowl along with the rest of the ingredients. Season to taste with salt and pepper, mix together and set aside.

To prepare the egg wash, crack the egg into a small bowl, add the rest of the egg wash ingredients, whisk together and set aside.

To assemble, fill a flat bowl with lukewarm water, dip a rice paper sheet in the water and, once soft and pliable, transfer to a clean work surface. Place a couple of tablespoons of the filling in the centre of the bottom half of the sheet. Gently pull the edge of the sheet away from the work surface and roll it over the filling, tucking it in firmly. Cut in half, fold in the sides and roll up tightly. Repeat with the rest of the sheets and filling. Transfer to the tray, brush with the egg wash and sprinkle with nigella seeds.

Bake for 20 minutes, or until golden and crispy. Once cooked, remove from the oven and set aside to cool completely. Wrap in parchment paper or reusable food wraps, and pack in a lunchbox along with the other items.

 A helping hand: *A child's task can be to whisk together the wash, brush the folded rice paper rolls and help with rolling them up.*

Potato, Pea and Spinach Tortilla

Makes 8 slices / Active preparation: 25 minutes / Start to finish: 40 minutes

Ingredients

3 tbsp butter, or olive oil
    or coconut oil
1 onion, peeled and finely chopped
350 g (12 oz) potatoes, rinsed
    or peeled and coarsely grated
2 handfuls (50 g/2 oz) of fresh
    spinach, stems removed and
    roughly chopped
150 g (5 oz/1 cup) frozen peas
8 eggs
sea salt and freshly ground
    black pepper

Other lunchbox items

sliced rye or gluten-free bread,
    spread with Chocolate chickpea
    spread (page 166)
fruit and veg salad (chopped
    tomatoes, carrots, celery,
    strawberries and blueberries)

Cold tortilla triangles served on the counter of every tapas bar in Barcelona are our children's favourite hand-held food when we are there. Our version is slightly simplified as we grate the potatoes instead of deep-frying them to cut the preparation time in half. We also add spinach and peas to pack in some more vegetables. But just like the traditional version, our tortilla triangles are great cold, can be eaten with your hands and are ideal in a lunchbox with a little side salad.

Preheat the oven to 250°C (500°F/gas 9) grill (broil) mode.

Melt a tablespoon of the butter in a large, preferably cast-iron, ovenproof, lidded frying pan (skillet), and sauté the onion over a medium-low heat for 5 minutes, or until the onion begins to soften. Add the potatoes to the pan along with one more tablespoon of butter and sauté for a further 5 minutes. Next, add the spinach along with the peas, season to taste with salt and pepper and sauté for a further 5 minutes, or until the onion has softened. While the vegetables are cooking, crack the eggs into a large bowl, season to taste with salt and pepper and whisk together.

When the vegetables are cooked, remove from the heat, add to the bowl with the eggs and gently fold together. Wipe the pan clean, put it back on the heat and melt the remaining butter. Pour the tortilla mixture into the pan, cover with a lid and cook for a few minutes. Remove the lid, transfer to the oven and grill for 7 minutes, or until golden and firm. Once cooked, remove from the oven and set aside to cool completely.

To assemble, cut into eight triangles, wrap in parchment paper or reusable food wraps, and pack in a lunchbox along with the other items.

 A helping hand: *Grating potatoes is boring so it's an excellent task for a child. Let them wear a ski glove to prevent them from cutting themselves and make the whole thing more fun and exciting.*

Banana Pancake Rolls

Makes 20 rolls / Active preparation: 10 minutes / Start to finish: 10 minutes

Ingredients

4 tbsp Chocolate chickpea spread
    (page 166)

4 tbsp cottage cheese

4 tbsp Berry and chia jam
    (page 161), or store-bought

4 tbsp almond butter (optional)

4 spinach pancakes (See rainbow
    pancakes recipe page 67)

4 bananas, peeled

We sometimes take our spinach pancakes, top them with Chocolate chickpea spread (page 166), berry jam and cottage cheese, roll around a banana and slice into hand-friendly rolls. They are perfect in a lunchbox and for small hands. The kids usually love these because they are sweet, but they also have a fair amount of nutritious value – so it's a double win! You can of course also vary the lunchbox with a few more savoury rolls as well.

Spread 1 tablespoon each of chocolate and chickpea spread, cottage cheese, berry jam and nut butter (if using) over each pancake. Place a banana on each filled pancake and roll the pancake around it into a log. Slice into hand rolls, place in a lunchbox and cover with parchment paper.

 A helping hand: *Peeling bananas is a good task for children – give them a small knife so they don't mash the banana too much. They can also help rolling the pancakes around the bananas, and filling the lunchbox.*

Seed Cakes with Carrot and Apricots

——— Makes 16 muffin-sized cakes ———

These muffin snack cakes are high in protein, easy to make and hold their shape well in a lunchbox. You can vary the flavours by subbing carrot and apricots for apple and raisins or beetroot and dark chocolate.

1. Measure out the ingredients: 200 g (7 oz/1 cup) cottage cheese, 400 g (14 oz/3 cups) mixed seeds (pumpkin, sunflower, flaxseeds, sesame), 4 eggs, 1 carrot, 6 dried apricots (unsulphured) and ½ tsp salt. And set the oven to 180°C (350°F/gas 4)

2. Peel and grate the carrot.

3. Use scissors to cut the apricots into bite-sized pieces.

4. Add all ingredients to a large mixing bowl.

5. Stir with your hands to combine.

6. Place muffin liners in a muffin tin and spoon the mixture into them. Smooth out the top with the back of a spoon. Bake for 20 minutes or until firm.

Snacks and
Drinks

———

Which vegetables have skins?

Which (bell) pepper colour do you think tastes best?

How many different vegetables have you eaten today?

What food can you pair with rice?

Do you dare to try a new vegetable tonight?

Three Veggie-packed Smoothies

Each recipe serves 2 / Active preparation: 5 minutes / Start to finish: 5 minutes

Fresh greens

50 g (2 oz/½ cup) frozen
    broccoli florets
1 banana or avocado, peeled
1 handful (25 g/1 oz) of fresh spinach,
    stems removed and roughly
    chopped
15 g (½ oz) fresh ginger root,
    peeled and grated
1 tbsp almond butter (optional)
125 ml (4 fl oz/½ cup) fresh
    unsweetened orange juice
125 ml (4 fl oz/½ cup) water

Cauliflower blues

125 g (4 oz/1 cup) frozen blueberries
1 banana (150 g/5 oz), peeled
½ avocado (75 g/2½ oz), stone
    removed and flesh scooped out
50 g (2 oz/½ cup) frozen
    cauliflower florets
2 soft dates, pitted
½ tsp ground cardamom
375 ml (12½ fl oz/1½ cups) milk
    of choice

Raspberry beets

1 beetroot (beet) (75 g/3 oz),
    top removed, peeled and grated
125g (4 oz/1 cup) frozen raspberries
4 soft dates, pitted
250 ml (8½ fl oz/1 cup) plain
    unsweetened yoghurt
125 ml (4 fl oz/½ cup) water
1 tbsp lemon juice

There simply is no easier and tastier way to give your kids an energy boost between meals (or for breakfast) than smoothies. They are quick to make, taste sweet and are portable. Many smoothies are just fruit-based, but we try to include healthy fats and fibres and also sneak in some vegetables. Here are three of our favourite veggie-packed smoothies.

Put all of the ingredients in a blender and mix until completely smooth. Taste and adjust the flavours to your liking. Pour into glasses and serve, or store in airtight bottles in the refrigerator to enjoy later.

 A helping hand: *Smoothies are great as a first step for kids in the kitchen as the method is so easy. Start by teaching them basic safety around a blender: never to stick their fingers into it, never to start it without their parents' supervision, and to always check that the lid is on. Let them peel bananas, chop fruit and veg, find the right ingredients in the freezer, pit dates, mix and taste.*

 Tip: *You can often replace banana with avocado if you prefer a less sweet smoothie. Although with kids that is usually not the case.*

 Note: *If you buy packs of frozen cauliflower or broccoli, they are usually pre-cooked or steamed before they are frozen so they can be added directly into the smoothie from the freezer. If you freeze your own vegetables, steam them first to make them easier to break down and digest.*

No-rice Pudding Jars

Makes 2 jars / Active preparation: 5 minutes / Start to finish: 5 minutes

No-rice pudding

125 g (4 oz/½ cup) plain
    cottage cheese
125 ml (4 fl oz/½ cup) plain
    unsweetened Turkish or
    Greek yoghurt
½ tsp vanilla extract

Raspberry jam bam

Berry and chia jam (raspberry flavour,
    page 161) or store-bought naturally
    sweetened raspberry jam (jelly)
nut or seed butter of choice
Cacao buckinis (page 173)

Apple sauce jar

Pure apple sauce (page 158)
    or store-bought unsweetened
    apple sauce
Chocolate chickpea spread
    (page 166)
roughly chopped toasted almonds
    or pumpkin seeds (pepitas)
ground cinnamon

These creamy jars imitate rice puddings but are made simply from thick yoghurt and cottage cheese and then a generous dollop of toppings. We usually keep them plain, but you could add in a dash of maple syrup if you prefer them sweeter. It's a great breakfast, snack or dessert that comes together in an instant. If you keep our chia jam or apple sauce in the refrigerator, these are made in a heartbeat.

To make the no-rice pudding, put the cottage cheese, yoghurt and vanilla powder in a medium-sized bowl, stir together and spoon into a jar.

To make the raspberry jam bam: Top the no-rice pudding with a few spoonfuls of the raspberry chia jam, a dollop of nut butter and a scattering of the cacao buckinis.

To make the apple sauce jar, top the no-rice pudding with a few spoonfuls of the apple sauce, a dollop of the chocolate and chickpea spread, a scattering of almonds and a sprinkling of cinnamon, or put an airtight lid on the jar and store in the refrigerator to have later.

 A helping hand: *You can teach your kids to make these jars themselves. It's super-easy to just stir together the yoghurt and cottage cheese and then top it with what they like.*

Banana Split Chia Bowls

2 large bowls or 4 smaller / Active preparation: 10 minutes / Start to finish: 25 minutes

Ingredients

6 tbsp chia seeds

500 ml (17 fl oz/2 cups) milk of choice

½ tsp vanilla extract

1 banana

2 tbsp dark chocolate (at least 70% cocoa solids)

2 tbsp cashew nuts

4 tbsp thick plain unsweetened Turkish or Greek yoghurt

2 tsp raw honey or maple syrup

2 tsp hulled tahini

Halved bananas, creamy yoghurt, chunky chocolate bites and crunchy nuts turn a basic chia pudding into a nutrient boosted version of banana split that you can spoil your kids with mid-day. Finish them with a drizzle of calcium-rich tahini and honey for extra sweetness. Chia seeds make the perfect base for snack recipes as they are nutrient packed and provide sustainable energy. We often prepare a big batch of chia pudding that we keep in the fridge so we can make these bowls in no time.

Put the chia seeds, milk and vanilla in a bowl. Give them a good whisk and set aside for at least 20 minutes, whisking once or twice in between to get rid of any lumps. The chia pudding is ready when it has thickened.

Meanwhile, prepare the topping. Peel the banana and cut it in half lengthways and then crossways. Coarsely chop the chocolate and cashews.

Spoon the chia pudding into bowls and top with the banana slices, yoghurt, chocolate and cashews. Drizzle with honey and tahini and serve.

 A helping hand: *Let the kids be in charge of whisking the chia seeds and milk, and of decorating the bowls.*

 Tip: *Stir a tablespoon of coconut cream into the chia pudding for a thicker and creamier texture.*

Dried Apple Rings, Two Ways

Active preparation: 15 minutes / Start to finish: 4 hours or 2–4 days

Ingredients

500 g (1 lb) apples, rinsed

1 tbsp ground cinnamon

Dried fruit makes for a great snack, and even if you can find various options in the supermarket, homemade have a cleaner ingredient list and are fun and easy to make. Apple rings are our kids' favourite choice of fruit. There are two methods to make these, either at room temperature for a few days, which gives you soft and chewy apple rings, or by roasting on a very low temperature in the oven for a few hours for crispier chips. All you need is seasonal apples and a good knife.

Core the apples and slice them thinly with a knife (or use an apple peeler/corer/slicer) to make rings. Dust with the cinnamon.

To making soft apple rings, thread the apple slices on long sticks or threads, making sure they don't touch one another, and hang to dry at room temperature. It can take 2–4 days, depending on the temperature, thickness of the slices and variety of apples. Taste every day to see if they are ready; they should be soft and chewy. Store them in an airtight glass container.

For recipes using two baking trays (pans), a fan-assisted oven gives the most even heat distribution. To make crispy apple chips, preheat a fan oven to 180°C (360°F/gas 4) or a conventional oven to 100°C (230°F/gas ¼). Line two baking trays (pans) with baking parchment. For recipes using two baking trays (pans), a fan-assisted oven gives the most even heat distribution. Arrange the apple slices in a single layer on the trays and bake for 3–5 hours. Turn them halfway through – this will help them dry out evenly and stay crisp for longer. When you remove them from the oven they should be dry but still slightly bendy; they will crisp up as they cool. Test if they are ready by removing one and letting it cool for a few minutes. Store them in an airtight glass container straight away.

 A helping hand: *A child can put the apple rings on a stick or a thread, and find good spots for them to hang.*

 Note: *If it's very warm and humid where you live, we recommend making the oven-dried version as otherwise the soft apple rings can go bad in the moist air at room temperature.*

Energy Bean Bars

Makes 12 bars / Active preparation: 15 minutes / Start to finish: 45 minutes

Ingredients

½ × 400 g (14 oz) tin kidney beans,
   rinsed and drained

14 soft dates, pitted

60 g (2 oz/¼ cup) virgin coconut oil

4 tbsp cacao powder, sifted

75 g (2½ oz/½ cup) pumpkin seeds
   (pepitas), preferably toasted

100 g (3½ oz/1 cup) rolled oats

50 g (2 oz/½ cup) desiccated
   (dried shredded) coconut

We keep various energy bars on rotation in our freezer. They're great for all 'post-' situations – post-workout, post-lunch, post-school, post-work or post-dinner. Many energy bars are pretty heavy on the sweet stuff, making them more of an indulgent treat rather than something substantial. So here we've added kidney beans to create a more balanced bar. They taste great and, together with the coconut oil, they keep your blood sugar levels stable, so you and your kids will be energised for longer.

Grease a 20 × 14 cm (8 × 5½ in) baking tray (pan) and line it with baking parchment.

Put the beans, dates, oil and cacao powder in a food processor, and blend until smooth, then transfer to a large mixing bowl.

Roughly chop the pumpkin seeds (pepitas) and add them to the bowl along with the rest of the ingredients and mix together.

Transfer to the pan and, with wet hands or the back of a spoon dipped in coconut oil, press down firmly so that it is even and compact.

Put in the refrigerator or freezer for 30 minutes, or until firm, before cutting into a dozen 7 × 3.5 cm (2¾ × 1⅓ in) bars.

Store in an airtight container in the refrigerator for up to a week, or for longer in the freezer; just thaw them ever so slightly before serving.

 A helping hand: *Let the kids help out with measuring the ingredients and adding them to the food processor. They can pit the dates and also help with pressing the mixture into the baking tray (pan).*

Sweet Potato and Spinach Muffins

Makes 12 muffins / Active preparation: 20 minutes / Start to finish: 45 minutes

Dry ingredients

1 sweet potato, peeled and
    coarsely grated
160 g (5½ oz/1¼ cups) buckwheat
    flour, sifted
100 g (3½ oz/1 cup) oat flour
2 tsp baking powder
1 tsp ground ginger
½ tsp sea salt

Wet ingredients

3 eggs
2 handfuls (50 g/2 oz) baby spinach
2 soft dates, pitted
180 ml (6 fl oz/¾ cup) plain
    unsweetened yoghurt
125 ml (4 fl oz/½ cup) olive oil
2 tsp lemon zest

Topping

75 g (2½ oz/½ cup) pumpkin
    seeds (pepitas)
2 tsp runny honey or maple syrup
1 tbsp olive oil
¼ tsp sea salt

Savoury muffins are brilliant for feeding youngsters as a great snack between meals. These muffins are packed with sweet potato and spinach and therefore have a round sweetness to them. We grate raw sweet potato instead of cooking it, making these quick and easy.

Preheat the oven to 200°C (400° F/gas 6). Grease a 12-hole muffin tin and line it with baking parchment or paper muffin cases. Alternatively, use a silicone muffin tin.

Put the sweet potato in a large bowl along with the rest of the dry ingredients. Stir together, make a well in the middle and set aside. Crack the eggs into a food processor, add the spinach along with the rest of the wet ingredients and blend until completely smooth. Pour the wet mixture into the well of the dry ingredients, gently fold together and set aside, making sure not to overmix, as the muffins will turn out tough otherwise.

To prepare the topping, put all of the ingredients in a small bowl, stir together and set aside.

Spoon the muffin batter into the prepared tin and top each muffin with a couple of teaspoons of the topping. Bake for 25 minutes, or until golden and springy, or until a skewer inserted in the middle of one of the muffins comes out clean. Remember to turn the tin around halfway through the cooking time to ensure that the muffins bake evenly. Once cooked, remove from the oven and set aside to cool slightly in the tin, before transferring to a wire rack to cool completely or devouring while still warm!

Store in an airtight container at room temperature for up to 3 days.

 A helping hand: *The kids can spoon the batter into the tin and dollop each muffin with the topping ingredients.*

Animal Grain Cakes

Makes 6 cakes / *Active preparation: 10 minutes* / *Start to finish: 10 minutes*

Ingredients

3 tsp smooth nut butter

6 plain puffed grain cakes (rice, corn, buckwheat, amaranth, quinoa)

1 avocado, stone removed and flesh finely mashed with a little lemon juice stirred through

2 small lettuce leaves

1 banana, sliced

1 apple, sliced

12 blueberries

4 strawberries, 2 halved and 2 sliced

5 raisins

2 thin slices of celery stalk

Let me tell you right away that we don't do animal-faced food on a stressful Tuesday morning when the kids are hungry and late for school. Nope, these cute little cakes have a different purpose (and time of the day). They are a crafty and fun way for our kids and their friends to play with food. And a method for us to show them that fruit and vegetables can have different textures, colours and shapes: 'What can we use as ears for the rabbit?' Getting children to reflect over food and think about it in new ways is almost as important as actually eating it. But with that said, it's usually a fight over who gets to eat these cakes as they are rather yummy too.

To make the rabbit, monkey and bear, spread the nut butter on half of the puffed grain cakes. To make the cat, dog and owl, spread mashed avocado on the remaining cakes. Then arrange fruit, berries and vegetables as pictured. Or follow your imagination and create new animals. Eat them straight away. If you're storing these in a lunchbox, you probably want to squeeze over a little lemon juice to prevent the fruit from turning brown, and expect the grain cakes to go a little softer instead of crisp, but kids usually don't mind.

 A helping hand: *If you prep the ingredients, the kids can create and decorate faces on the cakes themselves.*

Orange Bliss Balls

Makes 10 balls / Active preparation: 15 minutes / Start to finish: 15 minutes

Ingredients

75 g (2½ oz/½ cup) pumpkin seeds
  (pepitas)
40 g (1½ oz/¼ cup) sesame seeds,
40 g (1½ oz/¼ cup) flaxseeds,
15 soft dates, pitted
2 tbsp virgin coconut oil, melted
4 tbsp cacao powder, sifted
2 tbsp fresh unsweetened
  orange juice

To roll

hemp hearts or desiccated
  (dried shredded) coconut

We make these balls almost weekly and store them in the refrigerator for quick snacking situations and lunchbox treats. You don't need to follow an exact recipe, just add in any seeds or nuts or leftovers you have in the pantry. These are flavoured with orange and cacao and are super-popular with our kids.

Put all of the seeds in a food processor and pulse until the mixture resembles fine breadcrumbs. Add the rest of the ingredients and blend until the mixture comes together.

Working with a heaped tablespoon of mixture at a time, roll into 10 balls, about 30 g (1 oz) each, before rolling them in hemp hearts. The mixture will be quite soft and sticky to start off with, but once they are coated and refrigerated they will firm up nicely.

Store in an airtight jar or container in the refrigerator for up to a week, or for longer in the freezer; just remember to thaw them ever so slightly before serving.

 A helping hand: *Let your child help with pitting the dates, pulsing the food processor and rolling the balls in the hemp hearts.*

Snack Jars with Gold Dip

———— Makes 4 jars ————

Fruit and vegetable sticks with a dollop of peanut butter is a classic healthy snack and on lazy days we often just place a jar of peanut butter with a few carrots or apple slices on the table. This is a slightly upgraded version with a flavoured peanut butter dip that is served in a jar and then topped up with crunchy fruit and vegetables. Because it is so simple, you can let your kids make this on their own. Put a lid on the jar and they become a handy snack on the go.

1. Measure out all the ingredients: 125 g (4 oz/½ cup) peanut butter, 2 tbsp honey, 1 tsp freshly grated ginger root, ½ tsp ground turmeric, 4 carrots, 1 handful sugar snap peas, 3 celery stalks

2. Whisk together the peanut butter, honey and turmeric in a bowl. Add 2–4 tablespoons of water to thin the mixture as necessary.

3. Grate fresh ginger into the dip.

4. Trim the ends of the sugar snaps. Peel the carrots and cut them into sticks, along with the celery.

5. Scoop the dip into 4 mini jars.

6. Place the vegetables in the tahini filled jars and munch away.

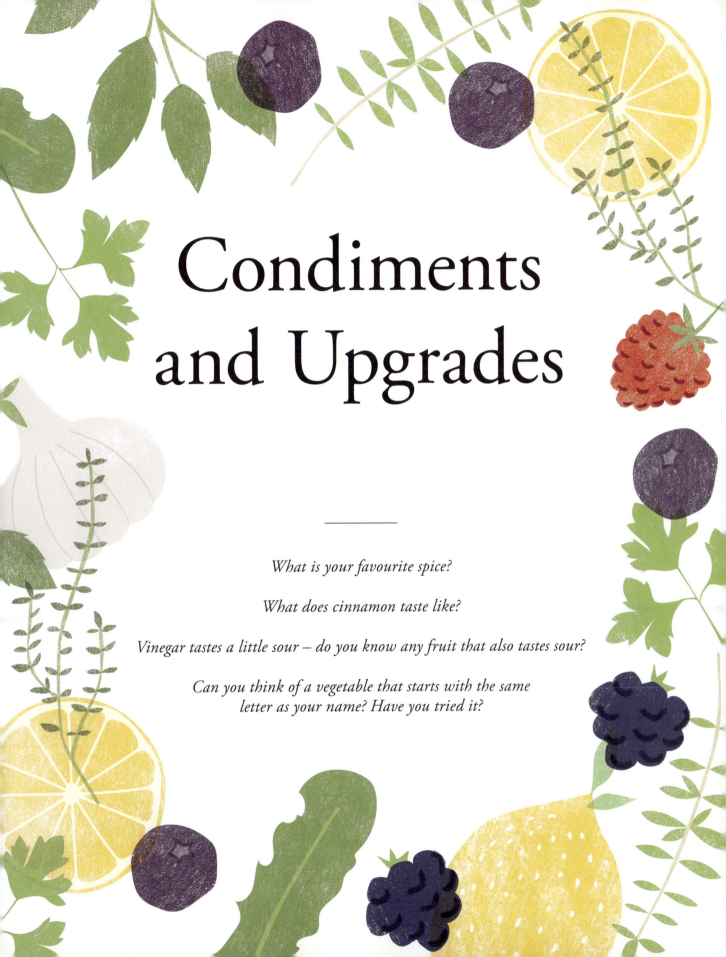

Condiments and Upgrades

What is your favourite spice?

What does cinnamon taste like?

Vinegar tastes a little sour – do you know any fruit that also tastes sour?

Can you think of a vegetable that starts with the same letter as your name? Have you tried it?

Pure Apple Sauce

Makes 750 g (1 lb 10 oz/3 cups) / Active preparation: 10 minutes / Start to finish: 30 minutes

Ingredients

125 ml (4 fl oz/½ cup) water

2 tbsp lemon juice

1 cinnamon stick

1 kg (2 lb) cooking apples,
    peeled and cored

A bunch of apples boiled into a sauce, with no sweetener and just a little lemon and cinnamon, is a great example of how the simplest things can be the best. It is tastier than anything you find in a store, has the freshest flavour and is perfectly sweet. Keep it in the refrigerator and eat within five days, but that won't be a problem. Add generous spoonfuls on top of porridge, cottage cheese jars (page 139), baked goods or sandwiches.

Put all of the ingredients, except the apples, in a large lidded saucepan. Cut the apples into bite-size pieces and add them to the pan. Bring to the boil, then reduce the heat and simmer with the lid ajar for 15 minutes, or until the apples are soft and cooked. Once cooked, remove from the heat and set aside to cool completely. Leave as is for a chunky sauce or mix with a hand-held blender until completely smooth.

Store in an airtight jar or container in the refrigerator for up to 5 days.

Berry and Chia Jams

———— Makes 300 g (10 oz/1 cup) / Active preparation: 5 minutes / Start to finish: 25 minutes ————

Ingredients

3–4 soft dates, pitted and mashed

80 ml (2¾ fl oz/ cup) water

250 g (9 oz/2 cups) frozen berries
(raspberries, strawberries,
blueberries, blackberries)

2 tbsp chia seeds

At the risk of sounding overly excited about something as common as a berry jam (jelly), this is a game-changer. Made with frozen fruit, only sweetened with dates and thickened with chia seeds, this takes three minutes to prepare and then a little more to thicken, and you can let the kids serve themselves in the morning without risking sugar overload.

Adapt the amount of dates to the sweetness of the berries. Sweeter berries like raspberries and strawberries need less and tangier berries like wild blueberries, blackberries or currants need a little more. You can also replace the dates with a glug of maple syrup if you prefer.

Put the dates in a small lidded saucepan along with the water and bring to the boil. Add the rest of the ingredients and stir together. Bring back to the boil, remove from the heat and set aside with the lid ajar for 15 minutes to thicken, stirring occasionally to prevent any lumps from forming. You can use a hand-held blender to make the jam smoother (especially for larger berries like strawberries or blackberries) or keep it chunkier.

Store in an airtight jar or container in the refrigerator for up to 5 days.

Fizzy Veg

———— Makes 1 large jar / Active preparation: 15 minutes / Start to finish: 5 days ————

You will need a 2 litre (70 fl oz) clean glass jar with rubber band and airtight lock.

Lacto-fermented cauliflower

1 cauliflower head
   (about 650 g/1 lb 7 oz)
   (see note below on other
   vegetable suggestions)
1 tsp mustard seeds
1 tsp fennel seeds (optional)
1 small garlic clove, peeled
20 g (¾ oz) Himalayan salt
1 litre (34 fl oz/4 cups) filtered water,
   at room temperature
1 cabbage leaf, to cover the top

Vegetables

You can ferment vegetables like carrots, cauliflower, green beans, broccoli, whole or quartered beetroots (beets), asparagus, onions, cabbage and garlic in a 2 per cent salt brine (20 g (¾ oz/1½ tbsp) salt to 1 kg (2 lb 4 oz) water). Cucumbers and peppers need a more concentrated salt brine to prevent mould, between 3.5 and 5 per cent salt.

Water and salt

It is important to filter the water as you want it to be free from chlorine and fluoride. The best salt to use for fermentation is pink Himalayan salt, as it is drier and good quality. Sea salt tends to hold moisture and can affect the weight of the salt. It can make the brine too high in salt and the product will end up without the healthy culturing probiotic lactic acid bacteria. Or it can make the brine too low in salt and the product will end up with moulds and yeast overgrowth.

Lacto-fermented vegetables go under the name 'fizzy veg' in our house. A type of healthy pickles, they are not only incredibly tasty but are also simple to make (even more so than sauerkraut) – you just need water, salt and vegetables (and spices). It takes a few days for the fermentation process to happen, but the sight of a four-year-old voluntarily snacking on a lacto-fermented cauliflower floret is so worth the wait.

The reason why they are so healthy is because of all the beneficial microbacteria that exist in these processes. They help keep your gut healthy, which is one of the keys to overall good health.

Prep the vegetables by gently rinsing, scrubbing and peeling, as necessary.

Break the cauliflower into small florets. Add the spices and garlic to the glass jar, followed by the cauliflower florets. Pack the vegetables tightly. Measure out the salt using a digital scale and then add it to the water and stir until completely dissolved. Pour the salt brine over the vegetables so they are fully covered. Leave a gap of 2.5–5 cm (1–2 in) at the top and place a whole folded cabbage leaf on top, to keep the vegetables submerged in the brine and prevent any oxidation. Close with an airtight lid. Leave at room temperature to ferment for about 5–10 days, depending on room temperature. It will become 'cloudy' after a day or so. The fermentation is complete when it's bubbling, has a vinegary aroma, tangy flavour and the veg is softer than raw but still has a bite. Remove the cabbage leaf and store the jar in the refrigerator.

 A helping hand: *Let your little ones break off the cauliflower florets. It's a good job for them as the florets don't have to be the same size.*

 Note: *Depending on what type of glass jar you are using, you might need to 'burp' the jar to prevent pressure building up. But if you use a lid with a silicone ring and an airlock system (like in the photo), the gases will be able to escape while keeping air out.*

 Tip: *If the salt brine doesn't cover completely, make another batch of 2 per cent salt brine as above and add extra brine until it covers completely. Discard the leftover brine.*

Carrot Krauts

——— Makes 1 kg (2 lb/6 cups) krauts / Active preparation: 25 minutes / Start to finish: 3 weeks ———

You will need a 1.5 litre (51 fl oz) glass jar with rubber band and airtight lock.

Ingredients

½ head (500 g/1 lb) white
    cabbage, washed

5 large carrots (500 g/1 lb), scrubbed

1 tbsp sea salt

1 tsp fennel seeds
    or 1 tsp caraway seeds

1 tbsp grated fresh ginger root

Fermented vegetables are the one type of food that we really recommend you introduce to your kids. It's gut-healthy food that boosts their immune system and is good on so many levels. If the thought of sauerkraut makes you fret, you probably haven't tried the real thing. It's fresh and tangy, can be made in a variety of flavours and colours, and all our kids love it (which we are eternally grateful for).

We use a technique called wild fermentation and it is the most natural way to do it, without any starters. It is super-simple and inexpensive; the only things you need are vegetables, salt and spices. And time – they need 2–4 weeks for the fermentation to be ready. If you want something quicker, try the Fizzy cauliflower on page 162.

Finely slice the cabbage (reserve a whole leaf to cover the top of the jar) and grate the carrots on a box grater. Or use a food processor with a fine slicer attachment for the cabbage and rough grating attachment for the carrots. Place all the ingredients in a large mixing bowl. Use your hands to knead and massage quite firmly until the vegetables are soft and juicy. They should release quite a lot of juice (vegetable brine); if not, just add a little more salt and keep on kneading. Use a spoon or tongs to lift the mixture into the jar. Pack it really tightly to squeeze out any air pockets, and keep packing until the jar is full of veggies and the veggies are covered in juice (important). Leave a little space at the top and place the reserved, folded, cabbage leaf there. This is to keep the krauts submerged in the brine and prevent any oxidation. Close with an airtight lid. During the fermentation process the veggies will expand and the liquid will try to come out – we put the jar in a bowl or a plastic bag to catch any juice that might drip from the sides. Leave the jar to ferment at room temperature for 2–4 weeks (depending on room temperature); 3 weeks is usually perfect. When ready, it should be softly textured but not mushy and have a fresh, spicy and acidic flavour. Discard the cabbage leaf from the top and store the jar in the refrigerator. We usually divide the fermented vegetables into smaller jars for easier serving and keep them in the refrigerator.

 A helping hand: *The hardest part of making krauts is kneading and massaging them so they release brine. Kids can help out with this – just make sure they have clean hands first. You can also hand them a pestle to pound the veggies with.*

 Tip: *If your veggies are stinky and leaky, place the jars in a bowl and cover with a closed plastic bag. Then place in a cupboard and drain the water from the bowl after about 3 days.*

 Note: *Use organic vegetables for fermenting and don't wash or scrub too much; it can destroy the natural enzymes on the vegetables.*

Chocolate Chickpea Spread

Makes 350 g (12 oz/1½ cups) / Active preparation: 10 minutes / Start to finish: 10 minutes

Ingredients

400 g (14 oz) tin chickpeas
    (garbanzos), rinsed and drained

8 soft dates, pitted

3 tbsp smooth peanut butter
    or hulled tahini

4 tbsp cacao powder, sifted

2 tbsp water or milk of choice

½ tsp sea salt

olive oil, to loosen (optional)

raw honey or maple syrup,
    for extra sweetness (optional)

For every spoonful of this creamy and super-tasty chocolate spread your kids eat, they also get chickpeas into their system. It only takes minutes to whizz together (much quicker than a nut butter), has no nasty ingredients and is great on top of our No-rice pudding jars (page 139), sandwiches, our Spinach and cottage cheese waffles (page 31) and pancakes. You should also try adding two tablespoons of this spread to a blender along with your favourite milk; mix on high speed for a few seconds and you have a super-lush and frothy chocolate milk (with chickpeas!).

Put all of the ingredients (except the oil and honey) in a food processor and blend until your desired consistency is achieved. If it is too thick to mix, you can add a little olive oil for a richer consistency or more water or milk. You can also add a little honey or maple syrup if you prefer it sweeter.

Store in an airtight jar or container in the refrigerator for up to 5 days (but it won't last that long!).

 Adult upgrade: *We like it best with tahini but the kids prefer the nuttiness from the peanut butter.*

 A helping hand: *Let the kids help with rinsing the chickpeas in water, adding everything to the blender and taste-checking the spread.*

Magic Green Sauce

Makes 225 g (8 oz/1 cup) / Active preparation: 10 minutes / Start to finish: 10 minutes

Ingredients

1 handful of mixed herbs, preferably
 flat-leaf parsley, coriander (cilantro)
 and mint, thick stems removed

½ avocado (75 g/2½ oz), stone
 removed and flesh scooped out

8–12 pickled jalapeño slices, drained

1 tbsp capers (baby capers), rinsed
 and drained

1 garlic clove, peeled (optional)

125 ml (4 fl oz/½ cup) extra virgin
 olive oil

2 tbsp lime juice

1 tsp apple cider vinegar

1 tsp maple syrup

½ tsp sea salt

A powerhouse of flavour with a balanced punch of tangy, spicy and sweet, this dressing transforms any regular salad to a taste bomb! We use this as an adult upgrade on many recipes in the book. It works wonderfully well with our Weekday Traybake (page 28) and is great inside our Portobello and avocado quesadillas (page 44). It makes the perfect dressing for the green beans in our Green soup with clouds of cream (page 55) and dipping sauce for our Rye empanadas with mushrooms and raisins (page 88).

Roughly chop the herbs, transfer them to a food processor along with the rest of the ingredients and blend until your desired consistency is achieved. Taste and adjust the flavours to your liking.

Store in an airtight jar or container in the refrigerator for up to 5 days.

Sunny Turmeric Tahini Dressing

Makes 350 ml (12 fl oz/1½ cups) / Active preparation: 5 minutes / Start to finish: 5 minutes

Ingredients

20 g (¾ oz) fresh ginger root, peeled

125 g (4 oz/½ cup) hulled tahini

2 tsp raw honey or maple syrup

1 tbsp ground turmeric

250 ml (8½ fl oz/1 cup) water

2 tbsp lemon juice

2 tsp apple cider vinegar
  (optional)

½ tsp sea salt

¼ tsp freshly ground black pepper

Here's another one of our favourite dressings. We literally drizzle it on top of everything – salads, quinoa, kale, eggs, sandwiches, the works! It's the perfect thing to keep in the refrigerator to give a kids' meal an adult upgrade.

Finely grate the ginger, transfer it to a blender along with the rest of the ingredients and whizz until completely smooth and frothy.

Store in an airtight jar in the refrigerator for up to a week.

Cacao Buckinis

Makes 50 g (2 oz/¼ cup) / Active preparation: 5 minutes / Start to finish: 10 minutes

Ingredients

4 tbsp buckwheat groats

1 tsp coconut sugar

1 tsp cacao powder, sifted

These are so simple to make and are a great substitute if you don't have granola at home. Just heat buckwheat for a couple of minutes in a pan with a little cacao and sweetener and you have a crunchy topping for breakfasts and snack jars.

Heat a small frying pan and dry-roast all of the ingredients over a medium-low heat for 5 minutes, or until golden and crispy, stirring from time to time.

Remove from the heat and set aside to cool completely. Store in an airtight jar or container at room temperature.

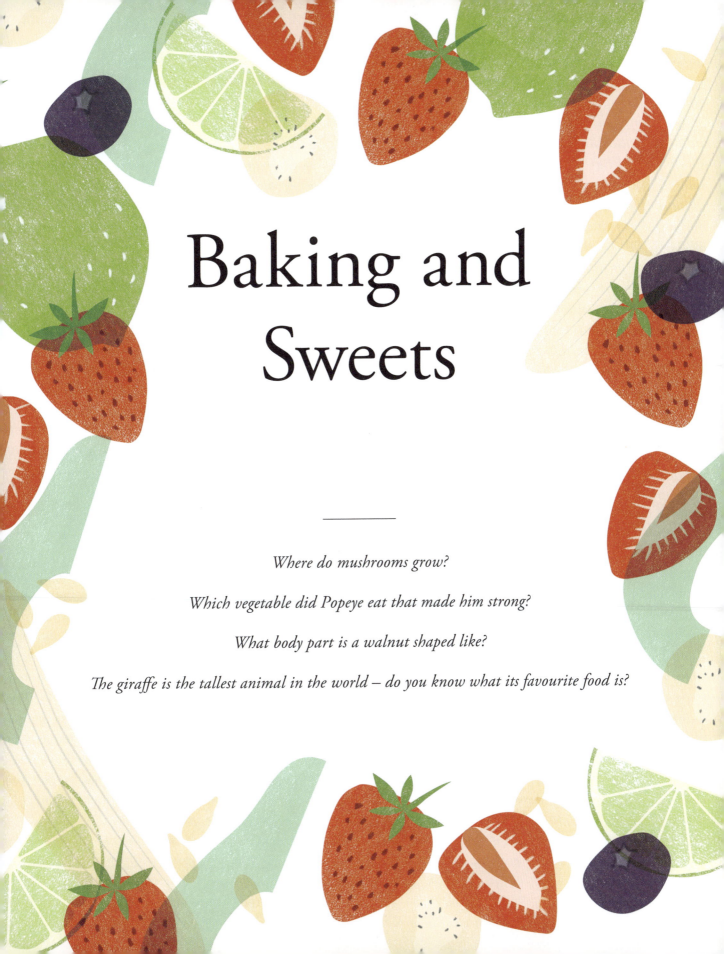

Baking and Sweets

Where do mushrooms grow?

Which vegetable did Popeye eat that made him strong?

What body part is a walnut shaped like?

The giraffe is the tallest animal in the world – do you know what its favourite food is?

Black Bean Brownie Bites

Makes 24 bites / Active preparation: 45 minutes / Start to finish: 1 hour

Wet ingredients

1 x 400 g (14 oz) tin black beans,
    rinsed and drained

20 soft dates, pitted

3 tbsp maple syrup (optional)

3 eggs

125 ml (4 fl oz/½ cup) olive oil

125 ml (4 fl oz/½ cup) milk of choice

Dry ingredients

50 g (2 oz/½ cup) (gluten-free)
    oat flour

50 g (2 oz/½ cup) almond flour

6 tbsp cacao powder, sifted

½ tsp baking powder

¼ tsp sea salt

75 g (2½ oz/½ cup) walnuts,
    preferably toasted (optional)

Mocha avocado frosting
(adult upgrade)

1 avocado, stone removed
    and flesh scooped out

8 soft dates, pitted

3 tbsp virgin coconut oil, melted

3 tbsp cacao powder, sifted

3 tbsp brewed espresso

To serve

whipped cream or plain unsweetened
    coconut yoghurt

halved strawberries

Beans are good for us, great even. So why not eat more of them?! We've tried a fair share of bean brownies and these are our favourite version. They're also very easy to make – just blitz everything in a food processor. They taste sweet but not overly so, but you can add a few tablespoons of maple syrup to the batter. We love to serve them with our mocha avocado frosting, but the kids like them best with just a dollop of whipped cream and half a strawberry on top.

Preheat the oven to 180°C (350°F/gas 4), grease a 28 × 20 cm (11 × 8 in) baking tray (pan) and line it with baking parchment.

To make the brownie bites, put the beans, dates and maple syrup (if using) in a food processor and blend until smooth. Crack the eggs into the food processor, add the rest of the wet ingredients and blend until smooth.

Add all of the dry ingredients to the food processor, except the walnuts (if using), and blend until smooth. Roughly chop the walnuts and stir through the mixture. Tip the batter into the prepared pan, spreading it out evenly, and bake for 30 minutes, or until springy and firm.

While the brownie is cooking, make the frosting. Put all of the ingredients in a food processor, blend until completely smooth and set aside.

When the brownie is cooked, remove from the oven and set aside to cool completely, before cutting into 5 cm (2 in) squares to make 24 bites.

Serve topped with a dollop of whipped cream and some strawberries, or store in an airtight container in the refrigerator for up to a week.

 Adult upgrade: *Serve with a dollop of the mocha avocado frosting and a sprinkling of sea salt flakes.*

 A helping hand: *If you add the ingredients to the food processor your child can be in charge of pulsing. Topping each brownie with a strawberry half is also a job cut out for small hands.*

 Vegan version: *Increase the amount of oat flour to 100 g (3½ oz/¾ cup) and replace the eggs with 80 ml (2¾ fl oz/⅓ cup) aquafaba (chickpea (garbanzo) brine) that you whip until soft peaks form and stir into the batter along with the walnuts. Bake for 40 minutes; it will be slightly stickier but firms up once it cools.*

Chocolate Oat Cookie Sandwiches

Makes 16 cookies/8 nice cream sandwiches / Active preparation: 20 minutes / Start to finish: 1 hour

Chocolate oat cookies

200 g (7 oz/2 cups) rolled oats

65 g (2¼ oz/½ cup) buckwheat flour, sifted

3 tbsp chia seeds

4 tbsp cacao powder, sifted

½ tsp sea salt

100 g (3½ oz/½ cup) virgin coconut oil or unsalted butter, melted

125 ml (4 fl oz/½ cup) maple syrup

60 ml (2 fl oz/¼ cup) milk of choice

Raspberry nice cream

2 frozen bananas (250 g/9 oz), pre-peeled and sliced

125 g (4 oz/1 cup) frozen raspberries

250 ml (8½ fl oz/1 cup) coconut cream (or double (heavy) cream)

¼ tsp peppermint extract (optional)

These are the best and simplest vegan cookies we've come up with so far. They're not as crumbly as other vegan cookies and therefore they're perfect to use for ice-cream sandwiches. You can, of course, use any store-bought ice cream, but we've thrown in this super-quick and easy three-ingredient, three-minute recipe that doesn't require an ice-cream machine and tastes the bomb!

For recipes using two baking trays (pans), a fan-assisted oven gives the mose even heat distribution. Preheat the oven to 200°C (400°F/gas 6) or a fan oven to 180°C (350°F/gas 4) and grease two baking trays or line them with baking parchment.

Stir the oats, flour, chia seeds, cacao powder and salt in a large bowl. Stir in the rest of the ingredients, and set aside for 30 minutes to thicken, stirring occasionally to prevent lumps. Roll into 16 balls, about 35 g (1¼ oz) each. Transfer to the trays and press down to form 8 cm (3 in) circles.

Bake for 15 minutes, or until golden and crispy. Once cooked, remove from the oven and set aside to cool completely on a wire rack. Store in an airtight jar or container at room temperature for up to a week.

To make the nice cream, put the bananas, raspberries, half of the cream and the peppermint extract (if using) in a food processor or blender and mix until smooth and creamy. Stop and scrape down the sides if needed and add more cream if it is too thick. Store in an airtight container in the freezer.

To assemble, thaw the nice cream slightly. Sandwich the cookies together with nice cream and smooth out the edges. Repeat with the rest of the cookies and nice cream. Devour straight away or store in an airtight container in the freezer thawing them ever so slightly before serving.

 A helping hand: *Let the kids roll the cookie dough into 16 balls and transfer them to the trays. With a little supervision, the kids can do all the steps in the nice cream recipe by themselves.*

 Tip: *If using store-bought ice cream, pick one that comes in a tube-shaped tub; that way you can place it on its side and cut right through the tub with a serrated knife to get perfect rounds.*

Frozen Banana and Chocolate Pops

—— Makes 4 large or 8 smaller / Active preparation: 15 minutes / Start to finish: 6 hours ——

You will need 4 or 8 wooden popsicle sticks

Ingredients

4 bananas

200 g (7 oz) milk or dark chocolate
(at least 70% cocoa solids)

150 g (7 oz/1 cup) toasted hazelnuts,
finely chopped

Frozen bananas dipped in chocolate are the ultimate child-friendly treat on a warm day. Super-easy to make, all natural, and they look fun too. We've sprinkled these with chopped hazelnuts, but you can use other nuts or seeds, desiccated (dried shredded) coconut or any sprinkles of choice. You can also dip and drizzle with peanut butter if you like. If making these for smaller children, you can cut the bananas in half and insert the popsicle sticks from the cut side to get eight smaller banana pops.

Find a tray or plate that can fit inside your freezer and cover with baking parchment.

Peel the bananas and carefully insert a popsicle stick into each one. Place them in a single layer on the tray or plate and freeze overnight, or longer.

When you want to eat or finish preparing the banana pops, melt the chocolate in a water bath and place the nuts in a shallow bowl. Dip and roll each banana in the chocolate, using a small spoon to help coat as much as possible, then quickly sprinkle with the chopped nuts, or toppings of your choice.

The cold banana will make the chocolate set quickly. Enjoy straight away or store them in the freezer for a month, or even longer.

 A helping hand: *Let your child sprinkle the nuts over the chocolate-dipped bananas. They can dip the bananas in the chocolate too, but you need to be rather quick to get a smooth result so nut duty is usually an easier task for little ones.*

Blueberry and Avocado Creamsicles

Makes 10 creamsicles / Active preparation: 15 minutes / Start to finish: 8 hours

Ingredients

2 avocados, stones removed
   and flesh scooped out
200 g (7 oz/1½ cups)
   frozen blueberries
10 soft dates, pitted
250 ml (8½ fl oz/1 cup) milk of choice
2 tbsp lime juice
150 g (5 oz/½ cup) nut butter
   of choice (optional)

A big fat yes to easy ice cream! These lovely 'creamsicles' are basically made of a thick smoothie that you freeze. They're ideal on warm summer days (and cold winter nights). You can vary them endlessly by adding your favourite fruit or berries; just remember only to use a little liquid and to add avocado to get that creaminess which differentiates them from ice lollies. Avocado also provides good fat and stabilises the sugar from the dates. We like to push nut butter in the middle of these as a rich and delicate surprise, but this step is entirely optional. We found our popsicle moulds on Amazon, but if you don't have any, small paper cups and popsicle sticks or teaspoons inserted in the middle work just fine. Simply tear off the paper when you want to eat them.

Put all of the ingredients, except the nut butter, in a blender and mix until completely smooth.

Divide the smoothie between 10 popsicle moulds and top each one with a tablespoon of the nut butter (if using).

Cover with the lid, insert the popsicle sticks, pushing the nut butter into the middle of the mould, and transfer to the freezer for 8 hours, or until frozen.

Devour straight away or store in the freezer to have later.

 A helping hand: *With a little supervision with the blender and the avocado stones, the kids can do all the steps in this recipe by themselves. You can tip the mixture into a smaller piped jug to make it easier for them to pour the smoothie into the moulds. Or they can use a spoon.*

Birthday Pancake Cake

——— Serves 8–10 / Active preparation: 1 hour / Start to finish: 1 hour 30 minutes ———

Ingredients

1½ × Rainbow pancake batter
(page 67 – omit the vegetable
add-ins)

Layers

500 ml (17 fl oz/2 cups) double
(heavy) cream or whipped coconut
cream (reserve half for topping
the cake)

250 g (8½/1 cup) runny almond butter
(or peanut butter) + 2 tbsp maple
syrup (or use the Chocolate
chickpea spread, page 166)

300 g (10 oz/1½ cup) Berry and
chia jam (page 161)

zest of 1 lemon

2 bananas, thinly sliced

1 tsp ground cinnamon

250 g (9 oz/2 cups) mixed berries
and physalis (thawed frozen
works too)

40 g (1½ oz) dark chocolate
(at least 70% cocoa solids),
grated or chopped

This has become the signature birthday cake of our family and one that we have been making since our daughter's very first birthday. It's fun to assemble and looks impressive with all the layers piled up. The pancakes and the layering can be done a day ahead and then topped and decorated just before serving.

You can easily vary the recipe by using different jams, adding cacao to the batter for a chocolate version or adding in other fruit.

Mix together the pancake batter and fry the pancakes. You need about 15 pancakes for this cake. Leave to cool completely before assembling the cake. Pour the cream into a bowl and use an electric whisk to beat until soft peaks form. (If you are making the cake a day ahead, only beat half of the cream and beat the rest for the topping the following day.) Stir together the runny nut butter and maple syrup in a bowl.

To assemble the cake, place the first pancake on a cake stand, then spread out a thin layer of the jam. Add a pancake on top and spread a layer of nut butter. Add a pancake and spread a layer of whipped cream and lemon zest. Add a pancake, spread out the banana slices evenly and sprinkle with cinnamon. Add a pancake and then repeat the layering sequence for about three more rounds. Top the last pancake with the reserved whipped cream, berries, physalis and grated chocolate. Finish off with cake candles and sing 'Happy Birthday'!

 A helping hand: *Let the kids help layering the cake and spread out the different fillings. Also let them decorate the top and place in the candles.*

Ruby Roll Cake

——— Serves 10–12 / Active preparation: 25 minutes / Start to finish: 50 minutes ———

Ingredients

8–10 soft dates, pitted

4 eggs, preferably free-range
and organic, separated

100 ml (3½ fl oz/ scant ½ cup) oat milk

1 beetroot (beet) (100 g/3½ oz),
peeled

100 g (4 oz/1 cup) almond flour

50 g (2 oz/½ cup) desiccated
(dried shredded) coconut

2 tbsp arrowroot (or potato starch
or cornflour/cornstarch)

½ tsp baking powder

pinch of sea salt

Filling

250 g (9 oz/1 cup) Berry and chia jam
(page 161)

250 g (9 oz/1 cup) mascarpone
(optional)

This retro cake has few ingredients, is naturally sweetened and comes with serious childhood flashbacks (at least for us). Our version is simple to make (and eat) and has been a success with the little ones. We've snuck a beetroot into the batter that gives it both character and colour. We fill it with mascarpone and any of our chia jams in the middle, but you can also skip the mascarpone and only opt for the jam if you want it dairy-free.

Preheat the oven to 180°C (350°F/gas 4) and line a large baking (cookie) sheet with baking parchment.

Put the dates in a food processor along with egg yolks and milk. Mix for a minute, or until the dates have dissolved and the mixture is lump-free. Grate the beetroot on a box grater (or use the grating attachment on the food processor). Add to the food processor and pulse until smooth and purple. Add the remaining cake ingredients (except the egg whites) and pulse until they all come together. Beat the egg whites in a separate bowl and, when they are fluffy, stir through the cake batter. Pour onto the baking tray (pan) and use a spatula to smooth it out evenly in a large rectangle over the paper. It should be roughly 30 × 35 cm (12 × 14 in) and about 1 cm (½ in) high.

Bake for 30 minutes, or until golden and a skewer inserted in the middle comes out clean. Meanwhile, stir together berry jam and mascarpone (if using). Take the cake from the oven and let it cool just slightly (it should still be a bit warm to make rolling easier). Carefully flip it upside down onto another sheet of parchment paper and peel the paper off the back. Slather the filling on top of the entire cake and roll it up like a sushi roll, using the parchment paper as a rolling mat. Serve it sliced up as hand rolls or plated with yoghurt and extra jam on top.

 A helping hand: *Kids can help out with most parts of this cake – pitting the dates, stirring the batter, flattening it out in the baking tray (pan) and, of course, slathering the filling on top.*

Jam and Sunflower Thumbprints

Makes about 15 cookies / Active preparation: 25 minutes / Start to finish: 40 minutes

Dry ingredients

125 g (4 oz/1 cup) finely chopped
    sunflower seeds

100 g (3½ oz/1 cup) rolled oats

65 g (2¼ oz/½ cup) buckwheat flour
    or plain flour

2 tbsp arrowroot (or cornstarch
    or potato starch)

1 tsp baking powder

½ tsp vanilla extract

pinch of sea salt

Wet ingredients

75 g (2½ oz) butter, at room
    temperature

80 ml (2¾ fl oz/⅓ cup) maple syrup

1 egg, separated

Topping

125 g (4 oz/½ cup) Berry and chia jam
    (page 161) or jam of choice

Baking with children always seems like the best idea when you start off. A lot of excitement from all parties. But somewhere between measuring out the flour and dropping an egg on the floor they start to lose interest. And soon you find yourself abandoned in the messiest kitchen with half-baked cookies and a kid jumping on a couch covered in flour. The key to success is choosing the right recipes and giving them enjoyable tasks – like with these cookies. They are quick and easy to put together and include a couple of fun jobs for the kids: using their thumbs to shape the cookies and then filling the craters with (too much!) jam.

Preheat the oven to 180°C (350°F/gas 4) and line a baking tray (pan) with baking parchment.

Spread out the sunflower seeds on the baking tray (pan) and roast for a few minutes until they look a little golden. Put half of the seeds in a food processor together with the oats and mix until you have a coarse flour. Add the rest of the dry ingredients (except the remaining sunflower seeds) to the food processor and pulse to combine. Use a hand-held mixer to beat the butter, maple syrup and egg yolk in a large bowl until light and fluffy. Add the dry ingredients to the bowl and mix until the dough comes together.

Scoop out about 15 portions of the dough and roll them between your hands into balls. If they crack easily you can add a splash of cold water to the dough. Whisk the egg white in a small bowl and coarsely chop the remaining sunflower seeds. Dip each dough ball in the egg white and then roll in the sunflower seeds. Place them on the baking tray (pan) spaced apart and use your thumb to carefully press into the middle of each cookie. Fill each indent with 1–2 teaspoons jam. Bake for 10–14 minutes, or until they look golden. Allow to cool slightly. They can be a little soft and fragile when warm, but firm up as soon as they cool down.

 A helping hand: *As mentioned above, these are great for kids to help out with. Let them press the food processor button, measure out the butter and maple syrup, roll the balls in the sunflower seeds, press their thumbs into the cookies and top them with jam.*

Salted Caramel Freak Shake

Makes 2 glasses / Active preparation: 15 minutes / Start to finish: 15 minutes

Shake ingredients

50 g (2 oz/½ cup) frozen
    cauliflower florets
1 frozen (pre-chopped) ripe banana
½ frozen (pre-chopped) avocado
    (75 g/2½ oz), or fresh
4–5 soft dates, pitted
good pinch of sea salt
250 ml (8½ fl oz/1 cup) coconut
    drinking milk or milk of choice
1 tbsp cacao powder
1 tbsp nut butter of choice

Topping

75 g (2½ oz) dark chocolate
    (at least 70% cocoa solids)
4 tbsp hazelnuts, finely chopped
100 ml (3½ fl oz/scant ½ cup)
    whipped coconut cream
    or regular whipped cream
1 tsp cacao powder
2 tsp peanut butter

Wait, what? This salted caramel shake is made using cauliflower and avocado!?

Yup, it's the ultimate Friday night shake and yet it contains ingredients that will keep blood sugar levels a little less freakish than regular milk shakes. We go all in with toppings, though, because drinking healthy-ish shakes should be fun!

Start by making the nut chocolate rims on the glasses. Melt the chocolate in a water bath or bain-marie and dip the rims of two glasses into the melted chocolate. Let the chocolate drip off and cool slightly and then sprinkle the nuts over the chocolate until entirely coated.

Dip a teaspoon in the melted chocolate and drizzle across the inside of the glasses to create a pattern (like in the photo).

Place the shake ingredients in a high-speed blender and mix until smooth; you might need to use a tamper or spoon to push down the ingredients or to add a little extra liquid – the goal is a thick, ice-cream-like shake. Taste and adjust the flavours.

Spoon the mixture into the glasses, then top with whipped cream, a sprinkle of cacao powder and a teaspoon of nut butter. Finally, drizzle with the remaining melted chocolate and scatter the remaining chopped nuts over the top.

Serve with a wide straw and a spoon.

 A helping hand: *We actually don't tell our kids that their shakes are spiked with cauliflower so you might be better off blending this yourself. Instead, let them help out with the topping – melting and drizzling the chocolate, whipping the cream and sprinkling everything on top.*

 Note: *If you buy packs of frozen cauliflower of broccoli, they are usually pre-cooked or steamed before they are frozen so they can be added directly into the smoothie from the freezer. If you freeze your own vegetables, steam them first to make them easier to break down and digest.*

 Tip: *Using a lot of frozen ingredients helps give the shake an ice-cream-like consistency, but you need a good high-speed blender. You can make it with an ordinary blender as well by replacing frozen bananas and avocado with fresh.*

Little Swedish Hoovers

———— Makes 16 mini hoovers / Active preparation: 35 minutes / Start to finish: 35 minutes ————

Green almond paste

1 handful (30 g /1 oz) of baby spinach

3 tbsp maple syrup (or honey)

200 g (7 oz/2 cups) almond flour

Chocolate filling

15 soft dates, pitted

150 g (5 oz/1 cup) cooked quinoa

50 g (2 oz/½ cup) desiccated
   (dried shredded) coconut

3 tbsp cacao powder

pinch of sea salt

80 g (3 oz) dark chocolate, melted

You can find this classic treat in pastry shops all over Sweden and Denmark. In Sweden, they are called hoovers because the filling was traditionally made from old cookie crumbs 'hoovered up' from the bakeries, then flavoured with arak, covered with a thin layer of marzipan and dipped in dark chocolate. That is probably also why they were shaped like old vacuum cleaners. These mini versions look remarkably similar but instead use leftover cooked quinoa (!) and dates in the centre and the marzipan is coloured with spinach. Perfect for a slightly healthier Swedish fika!

To make the almond paste, put the spinach, maple syrup and half of the almond flour into a food processor and blend to dissolve the spinach. Add the remaining flour and mix until it comes together into a firm green ball. Take it out of the food processor and place in a bowl in the fridge while making the chocolate cake mixture. Clean the food processor.

To make the chocolate filling, put all the filling ingredients into the food processor and blend until combined. Taste and adjust the flavours. Divide into two equal-sized balls and roll each into 2 cm (¾ in) thick and 40 cm (16 in) long logs. They will be a little sticky but it doesn't matter as they will be covered in almond paste.

To assemble, place the almond paste between two baking papers and use a rolling pin to roll it out into a long and thin rectangle, roughly 40 x 20 cm (16 x 8 in) and 3 mm (⅛ mm) thick. Cut the rectangle length into two long strips. Place the two chocolate logs on each marzipan* strip and roll the almond paste tightly one lap around each log, cut off any remaining almond paste and use your fingers to pinch the edges together so you have two long green cylinders. Cut into 5 cm (2 in) pieces and place on a plate with the pinched-side down. Let cool in the fridge while melting the chocolate in a water bath.

Dip both ends of each log in chocolate, let any excess drip off and place the logs back on the parchment paper to set. When the chocolate is firm, they are ready. Store in the refrigerator for up to five days.

 A helping hand: *The marzipan can be a little tricky to get even and thin but let the kids roll out the filling and dip the ends in chocolate.*

 Tip: *You can add arrak essence, peppermint oil, cinnamon or coffee to the filling for a twist in flavour.*

*If the marzipan is sticky to handle, you can dust with a little potato starch or cornstarch.

Mini Raspberry Cupcakes

Makes 24 mini cupcakes or 12 regular / Active preparation: 25 minutes / Start to finish: 40 minutes

Dry ingredients

100 g (3½ oz/1 cup) almond flour

120 g (5 oz/¾ cup) rice flour

45 g (1¾ oz/½ cup) desiccated
 (dried shredded) coconut

2 tsp baking powder

1 tsp freshly ground cardamom

1 tsp vanilla extract

1 pinch salt

Wet ingredients

14 soft dates (150 g), pitted (if using
 dried dates, soak them for an hour)

1 ripe banana, peeled and cut into
 large chunks

4 tbsp coconut oil or butter,
 at room temperature

180 ml (6 fl oz/¾ cup) plain
 unsweetened yoghurt

3 eggs

24 raspberries (fresh
 or thawed frozen)

Berry Frosting

70 g (½ oz) raspberries
 (or strawberries), fresh
 or thawed frozen

3-4 soft dates, pitted

200 g (7 oz) cream cheese

These mini muffins are really delicious and moist with hints of coconut, banana, almonds and cardamom. It's one of our go-to recipes that we change slightly every time. They are only sweetened with fruit and entirely gluten free, yet they are sweet and have a delightfully soft crumb. If you are allergic to nuts, you can replace the almond flour with 100 g (3½ oz/ ½ cup) toasted sunflower seeds that have been ground into a flour.

Preheat the oven to 200°C (400°F/gas 6). Grease a 24-hole mini muffin tin (or 12-hole if making regular) and line it with baking parchment or paper muffin cases. Alternatively, use a silicone muffin tin.

Place all of the dry ingredients in a bowl, stir together and set aside. Add the dates to a food processor and blend on high speed. When smooth, add the banana and coconut oil and blend again. Finally, add the yoghurt and eggs, then blend until smooth and thoroughly combined. Pour the wet ingredients into the bowl with dry ingredients and stir together. Drop the batter into the muffin tins, then place 1-2 raspberries in the centre of each muffin and cover with some more batter. Bake for 10-12 minutes for mini cupcakes (or 17–20 minutes if making regular ones) or until golden and just set.

Prepare the frosting while the muffins are in the oven. Mix the raspberries and dates in a food processor or with a hand-blender until completely smooth. Whisk the berry mixture together with the cream cheese in a medium-sized bowl until pink and smooth. Scoop the frosting into a piping bag. Place it in the refrigerator for at least 20 minutes to firm up.

Let the muffins cool completely before piping the frosting on top. Serve immediately or store in the fridge.

 Vegan version: *For a vegan version soak 3 tbsp chia seeds in 9 tbsp water for 15 minutes, stir around and use instead of the eggs. And use a plant-based yoghurt and cream cheese.*

Apple Cake in a Glass

—— Serves 4 ——

This is a twist on an old-fashioned Danish apple cake, which curiously isn't a cake at all, but more like a very simple trifle. The apple sauce can be made at home (recipe on page 158) or use a good unsweetened store-bought version. This is an easy recipe that kids can make on their own, often leaving a proud grin on their faces and a mess of cream and apple sauce splattered on the table, walls and floors.

1. Measure out the ingredients: 4 dates, 250 g (9 oz/1 cup) apple sauce, 250 ml (8½ fl oz/1 cup) double (heavy) cream, 20 walnuts, 1 tsp ground cinnamon.

2. Pit the dates, place them on a cutting board and use a fork to mash them into a paste. Chop the walnuts.

3. Combine the chopped nuts and date paste into a sticky crumble.

4. Pour the cream into a bowl and whisk on high speed until medium stiff peaks form.

5. Spoon 4 tablespoons apple sauce each into four glasses. Add the date crumble on top and then the whipped cream.

6. Top with a sprinkling of cinnamon and serve.

ABOUT THE AUTHORS

David Frenkiel and Luise Vindahl are the couple behind the award-winning
vegetarian food blog Green Kitchen Stories and popular Instagram accounts.
They have followers from all over the world and have been leading the
path for greener eating habits for the past 10 years. Healthy, seasonal and
delicious vegetarian family recipes paired with colourful and beautiful
photographs have become the trademark of their style. They are the authors
of several internationally acclaimed cookbooks, *The Green Kitchen* (2012),
Green Kitchen Travels (2013) and *Green Kitchen Smoothies* (2015) and *Green
Kitchen at Home* (2016), all published by Hardie Grant UK. This
is the couple's fifth cookbook.

David and Luise's work has appeared in *Food & Wine Magazine, Bon
Appetit, ELLE, Vogue,* the *Guardian, National Geographic* and many more
publications. In 2013 and 2015 their blog was awarded in the Saveur
Magazine Best Food Blog Awards. They have also released two best-selling
apps for iPhone and iPad.

Luise is Danish and David is Swedish. They currently live in Stockholm
with their daughter Elsa and sons Isac and Noah. Apart from doing freelance
recipe development and food photography, David works as a freelance
graphic designer and Luise is a qualified nutritional therapist.

Read more on www.greenkitchenstories.com
@gkstories
@luisegreenkitchenstories

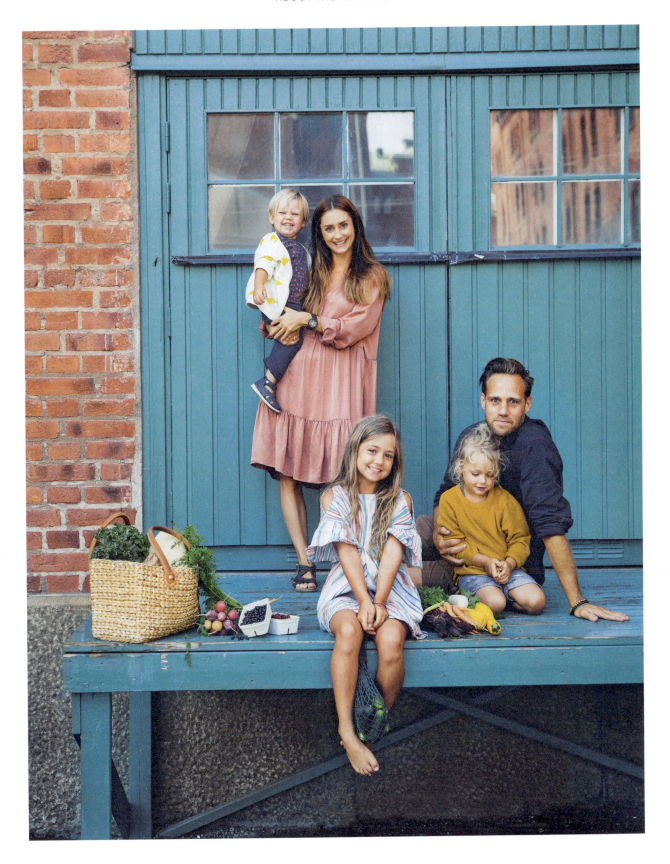

ACKNOWLEDGEMENTS

A big kiss to our three monkeys, Elsa, Isac and Noah. Satisfying your taste buds will always be our biggest challenge and motivation. Maybe you will stumble over this text in a couple of years. You were such a big part in the making of this book; tasting all the food – sometimes happily and other times hopelessly disappointed – and giving us (sometimes not so) constructive feedback, helping us holding bowls for photos and eating the same dinner for a third day in a row because we needed to perfect a recipe. Totally understandable if you are a little tired of these dishes for a while now.

A massive hug to Nicola Moores and and Sophie Mackinnon. You have both been with us for a couple of books now to help give us perspective, feedback and relieve some of the worst stress. Thank you Nic for testing all the recipes in this book (except from a few last-minute additions), for making them easier to understand, more consistently written, for letting us know when something isn't good enough (bye bye popcorn salad), for suggesting new recipe names when we have lost inspiration and for providing endless pages of feedback.

Thank you Sophie for assisting us in so many parts of the cookbook process. You came in when this book was just a baby. We had a couple of intense weeks where we put the heart and soul of the book together. You also helped us shop ingredients, write planning lists, prepare food during shoots, assist with the styling and stay focused and positive. Hope to see you in Stockholm again soon.

Thank you Molly, Kate, Stephen and the rest of the crew at Hardie Grant for giving us the opportunity to write our FIFTH book together. We really love working with all of you. Even when we had to push delivery dates and do last-minute recipe changes you stayed patient. We are so amazed by the trust and confidence you give us.

Thank you Stuart for designing this book and making those beautiful illustrations.

Thank you Uncle Sven for letting us stay at your stunning summer house to shoot part of this book.

Thank you to our beloved families in Denmark and Sweden, for playing with the kids while we work on the weekends, for following us on this journey and for encouraging us in every crazy step we take off the normal path. We love you.

Finally, a massive and heartfelt thank you to all of you who have been reading our blog, Green Kitchen Stories, and following our journey for the past 10 years. None of this would have happened if you hadn't been there, cheering us forward, writing friendly notes and comments, spreading likes and buying our books. You changed our lives and made all this possible. We are forever grateful.

Little Green Kitchen

Published in 2019 by Hardie Grant Books,
an imprint of Hardie Grant Publishing

Hardie Grant Books (London)
5th & 6th Floors
52–54 Southwark Street
London SE1 1UN

Hardie Grant Books (Melbourne)
Building 1, 658 Church Street
Richmond, Victoria 3121

hardiegrantbooks.com

British Library Cataloguing-in-Publication Data. A catalogue record
for this book is available from the British Library.

ISBN: 978-1-78488-227-3

10 9 8 7

Publishing Director: Kate Pollard
Senior Editor: Molly Ahuja
Junior Editor: Eila Purvis
Cover and Internal Design: Stuart Hardie
Illustrations: Stuart Hardie
Editor: Lorraine Jerram
Proofreader: Wendy Hobson
Photography ©: David Frenkiel
Recipe tester: Nicola Moores
Indexer: Cathy Heath

Colour Reproduction by p2d
Printed and bound in China by Leo Paper Products Ltd